HENRY JENKINS   ROBERT V. KOZINETS

BOOK 1:

DEFINING FANDOM

The Frames of Fandom Series

GATEWAY
PLANET PRESS

Founded in 2024, Gateway Planet Press is committed to publishing innovative and useful knowledge that reaches beyond the confines of traditional academic presses. Our mission is to deliver accessible, affordable, and high-quality research and teaching resources to scholars, professionals, and curious readers worldwide. By embracing new technologies and fresh perspectives, we seek to foster understanding, inspire critical thought, and, where necessary, spark meaningful change. This is just the beginning. Many journeys are possible—let us be your gateway.

GATEWAY PLANET PRESS

Gateway Planet Press
Los Angeles, California

Defining Fandom: Book 1 in the Frames of Fandom Series was
Edited by Emily Lisa Thorntom
Formatted by Dawn Black
Indexed by Henry Jenkins and Robert V. Kozinets
Cover Designed by Robert V. Kozinets, Henry Jenkins, and ChatGPT4o
Final Cover Art by Robert V. Kozinets

ISBN: 979-8-9910913-2-9

FRAMES OF FANDOM:
The Book Series

TABLE OF CONTENTS

PREFACE:
Welcome to Book 1

Gone are the days when fandoms were relegated to the fringes of pop culture. Today, fandoms are thriving, woven into the webwork of our collective conversation and experiences, profoundly interlinked with our identities, and influencing many of the choices we make. They include, but also transcend, sports and entertainment franchises to encompass the full spectrum of activities and interests with which many people passionately engage.

Welcome, Gentle Reader, to this book, **Defining Fandom**, which is the first in a series about the multifarious worlds of fandom. The ancient etymology of the word multifarious implies something that is strong, great, and numerous. We find these qualities in fandom and have found that fandom takes many different forms and has numerous parts and elements. Throughout these books, we explore, explain, and find delight in these diverse and varied manifestations of fans and fandoms. To understand them, we adopt a series of different conceptual perspectives, viewpoints, or frames.

The 15-book series is called **Frames of Fandom.** Each book is self-contained, which means that the books can be read separately or in any order. However, there is an intentional logic and flow that makes reading them in sequence the optimal experience. The books that follow this one should not be read as the constituent elements of some academic treatise. It might be fitting to release an episodic book series reminiscent of the serial formats under which many of the original fan tales, like Sherlock Holmes or Batman, were published. However, this is not the case. Instead, readers should view **Frames of Fandom** as a collection of stories and conceptual connections that try to bring to life the captivating world of fandoms and then explain that realm using the most sophisticated theories and methodologies currently available. We do so by using a series of frames (ways of understanding) through which to think about what kind of community a fandom is and how it relates to the popular culture around which it organizes. We celebrate the collectives that have emerged, the impact they wield, and the potential they hold.

Each book focuses attention on a particular paradigm that scholars have used to understand some dimension of fandom. These frames may be overlapping, as in the case of, for example, **Fandom as Co-Creation** and **Fandom as Participatory Culture**. Both explain fandom as a site of cultural production, the first from the perspective of industry and within the field of consumer research, the second from the perspective of the fan and within the theoretical traditions of cultural studies. Sometimes, one frame—say, **Fandom as Public**—provides the preconditions for the second—**Fandom as Activism**. In some cases, the relationship between the two is harder to nail down, as is the relationship between the focus on affect in **Fandom as Desire** and religion in **Fandom as Devotion**. However encyclopedic this project's scope may seem, the range of frames here is not exhaustive. However, we try to capture most of the dominant paradigms in the field.

Defining Fandom is the first book in the series. **Defining Fandom** provides useful conceptual grounding and introduces the auto-ethnographic style of the series, which draws heavily from the aca-fan tradition and the work both authors have written in that modality. Fans are people who passionately engage with their "fan object," which is not a physical object per se but a media or consumer culture production like BTS, *Deadpool,* or the Dallas Cowboys that becomes an object of their attention and affection. The fan's passionate engagement is called fanship, and some people's fanship becomes social, involving people such as friends and family. Fanship becomes membership in a fandom when a fan joins a collective of other fans of a shared fan object and partakes in participatory culture. Being a fan and partaking in fanship are personal states or identities; being in fandom is a social affiliation. Fandoms comprise some of the most passionate, connected, creative, critical, and/or active fans. Fandoms give them an outlet through which they celebrate, support, critique, reimagine, and derive pleasure from the activities related to their fan object. These important definitions are illustrated and developed in this book and they serve as the foundation upon which we build and expand the series.

Defining Fandom also overviews the coming series of books. When you see a bolded title, such as **Fandom as Audience**, **Fandom as Subculture**, or **Locations of Fandom**, this is meant to signify the title of another volume in the series. Throughout this book and the others, we will be referring to these titles as if they are all already published. Because we are publishing them on a staggered schedule, not all of the books we refer to may yet be available, but they have all been drafted (if not finalized) at the time of this release. Eventually, we will have all of the books we mentioned available to you and this book will accurately reflect the entire series.

Goals of this Book Series

As we embark on our journey through the frames of fandom, please keep in mind that we do so with three purposes in mind. The first is an intellectual one. The book series seeks to develop the synergies between Henry's world of fandom studies and Rob's world of marketing and consumer research. Both fields draw on tools and models from cultural anthropology to explain how everyday people operate within a consumer economy and in relation to the media industries. This would seem to provide common ground for us to learn from each other. In fact, we have been exchanging ideas with each other for almost 30 years.

The second purpose, interrelated with the first, is to inform various practices. Marketers, brand managers, and industry professionals increasingly need to understand and work with fandoms. Understanding the passionate engagement behind fandom makes amazingly good sense from a business perspective. Yet managers who dive for treasure in the shark-infested social media backwaters of brand-fan interactions know that working with fans is a high-risk, high-reward task often fraught with peril. Our core advice – Above all, do no harm. We are not trying to teach you how to exploit fandom. Quite the opposite, we want to teach you how to build a constructive relationship that respects and values the existing relationship between fans and any fan objects you may be working with.

There are also practitioners on the fandom side: the fans themselves and those who assist them. Fandoms are interrelated but also independent organizations from corporations and individuals who manage the objects of their fandom. Fans and fandoms sue companies, are sued by them, or sue each other. Fandoms are financially important. We also believe that they are culturally important.

We have both been working with organizations in these areas for decades, and our combined experiences lead us to believe that we can provide valuable information to better guide businesses and organizations alike—this is practical knowledge. Being useful requires us to blend the academic rigor of fan studies and consumer research with the pragmatic insights of brand management and marketing strategy.

The third purpose is to build on, promote, and try to further the new and important field of fandom relations. In both of our native academic fields—marketing and consumer research as well as communication and fan studies—researchers had long sent back signals that consumers were far from the passive dupes, observers, and recipients that earlier theories and assumptions had made them out to be. Instead, fans, fandoms, consumers, and consumer collectives were enmeshed in complex and passionate relationships with the brands and franchises that shaped their lives.

We see the **Frames of Fandom** series as more than explanatory literature, more than a business guide, and more than a source of inspiration for fan organizations. To match the reality of fandom today, we offer you a series that may shatter categories. We believe it breaks new ground on almost every page and reflects our insights about building bridges between our respective fields. It is not a rehash of established wisdom but rather a consolidation of original and, in some cases, controversial thinking.

About this Book and its Authors

Most students could not name the authors of their textbooks. We assume that the textbook's author is an "expert." The faculty teaching the books surely knows who the authors are. But the textbook author's role is to write in a neutral voice, summarizing what the field knows rather than sharing the objects of their own passion and curiosity. They are not trying to make an original contribution. Their personalities are masked: most textbooks bore us to tears. They could have just as easily been written by artificial intelligence. Such prose seems lifeless to our eyes and seems inappropriate for the topic of fans and fandom, which is all about passion and personal investments. The field of fandom studies has long focused attention on the positionality of the researcher—that is, our relationship to the objects of our study.

This book grew from two lifetimes of conversations with media, family and friends, other fans, other scholars, and, perhaps most centrally, conversations with each other. As we are about to relate to you, we've recently had the privilege of developing those conversations much further while teaching a course called Fan Relations, which we designed together at the University of Southern California's Annenberg School for Communication and Journalism.

The resulting books constitute an ongoing conversation about the intersection of fan studies and marketing. We have been talking about how to bring that conversational quality to the book, and what you are reading is the result. Many multi-authored books hide the individuality of their authors, but it seemed like there was no way to do that with this book and no need to. The two of us have distinct voices, but the conversations we have always had were about bringing our viewpoints together into something new.

You may have noticed that this book series is self-published by the authors on Amazon. Although we have a wealth of experience working with academic publishers, we have been less than satisfied with our ability to get our message out in forms that were appropriate to us and our readers. We offer these books at a reasonable price and in a slim form that would have likely been impossible for us to arrange with a traditional academic publisher. As a further benefit, we could take control of book marketing and also, potentially, more fairly compensate ourselves for our efforts.

You may find one of our voices stronger than another in any given book or passage, reflecting where these different conceptual frames come from. However, we both contributed to every text in this series. In order to continually signal our stakes in this research, we are, at times, holding onto the first person to describe our own experiences and insights. Where this happens, look for the phrase "Rob Here" or "Henry Here" at the start of a subchapter. In other places, we simply refer to ourselves as "we" and offer our work in the third person. We hope this doesn't become too confusing.

Henry and Rob have both fan and professional interests in the topics discussed. One or another of us maintains social relations with most of the other scholars we reference here. They are our mentors, students, colleagues, and friends. We have learned from them, and they have drawn on our research within the network of knowledge production that constitutes any academic field. This is especially the case with fields like fandom studies and consumer culture theory and research, which are relatively small by disciplinary standards. Although we will be discussing what we see as some key strands of research within our respective fields, we process them through the lenses of two lifetimes of active research and active participation within fan communities.

And now, we invite you to read and enjoy our exploration of the multifarious worlds of fandom with the first book of this series: **Defining Fandom**.

CHAPTER 1:

Rob: A Fan's Life

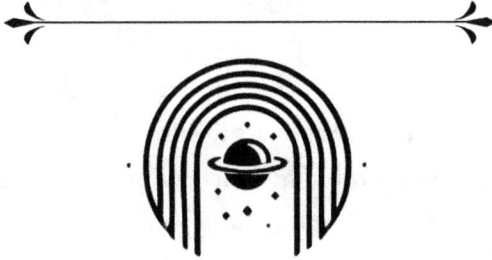

Auto-ethnographic Beginnings

ob here. Auto-ethnography is a form of qualitative research where the researcher uses their own personal experiences as their jumping-off point for explorations of broader understandings. Researchers engaging in auto-ethnography will often reflect on significant experiences from their own lives, analyzing and interpreting these events in the context of relevant cultural and societal frameworks and using them to shed light on larger human conditions. Advancing thinking about fandom requires more than the simple recitation of what others, or even ourselves, have said. I firmly believe that it means introducing introspective data about our own experiences and using it to build on what we already know. In fact, initiated by Henry's *Textual Poachers*, much of the fan studies literature has adopted the auto-ethnographic style. Auto-ethnographies tend to make for vivid storytelling within the scientific paradigm. They are not without their problems or critiques, however. As David Hayano (1979) wrote, "in many ways, the problems of auto-ethnography are the problems of ethnography compounded by the researcher's involvement and intimacy." Henry and I will keep these critiques in mind as we develop the ideas from our auto-ethnographic beginnings, adding to them a wealth of other information and research to give our work a properly scientific tone. But we will be trying to maintain where and when we can, our own involvement, experiences, and sense of intimacy with the worlds of fandom.

Apart from the fact that my identity as a fan and participation in fannish events and activities has appeared sporadically in various research contexts that I have investigated over the years, I've never written specifically before about my life as a fan or a fan-scholar. Although Henry and I thought that having a personal, first-person perspective on our own fandoms was going to be a key part of this book, I still feel a bit exposed writing about the role of fandom in my life in this way, so please bear with me through the awkwardness.

Early Role of Family

What could be more intimate than family, and family is at the core of my initial fandom, without a doubt. This is a portrait of 11-year-old me, drawn by Frank Kelly Freas, a renowned science fiction artist. At that age, my father used to take me, often with a select friend, to science fiction and comic book conventions around Toronto. I was deeply into my fan interests at that age and very fortunate to have a father who supported and sometimes shared them. The story behind the portrait was that there was a lottery to have Freas draw your portrait. I entered, but didn't win. We were waiting with the artist for the person who had won the draw to show up. My dad was chatting with him. Freas, who was a very nice man, asked me if I wanted him to draw my portrait while we waited for the winner to show up and, of course, I said yes.

It was a big advantage to have a father who was a traditional literary fan. My father had a huge collection of books by Edgar Rice Burroughs, about Doc Savage, Perry Rhodan, and others. Probably because he embraced them as a kid, he loved pulp style varieties of fantasy and science fiction, and I grew up watching him devour books and eagerly watch television programs. He was athletic, loved playing sports, and watched some sports, especially baseball. He also clearly enjoyed inhabiting his own imaginary worlds populated by the likes of Tarzan of the Apes, James Bond, and John Carter of Mars, even at times playfully embodying Tarzan's bare-chested thumping or James Bond's flirtatious punning. He was definitely fannish, although he was not involved in the social side of fandom. He dove into different book series with great enthusiasm, reading through most of the authors that he liked. It is almost impossible to think of my own fandom without connecting it to the activities of my father.

My mother was an active accomplice as well. Another bibliophile, she invested innumerable hours reading me stories, many of them fantasies, answering my endless questions about them, and watching movies with me and my sister.

There were so many childhood books I was attached to that I still can recall. I was dazzled by the "darkness and light" origin story and characters of Mattel's *Upsy Downsy Land* (Mattel, 1969)—a story that Wikipedia today calls "surreal" and "slightly psychedelic" (thanks, Mom). I vividly remember playing with the gyroscopic Wizzers from that mythical world.

And, like many North American children, I was raised on a steady diet of Disney mini-books (many of them Little Golden Books), Read Along books with records, and movies, and we regularly tuned in to *The Wonderful World of Disney* on TV. My mom took us to *Disney on Ice*. Every other winter, our family would spend three days driving from Toronto to Orlando to experience a biennial pilgrimage to Disney World. Those pilgrimages, which began when I was 8 years old, further cemented my fascination with the entire Disney enterprise, especially the imagineering that went on behind the scenes. When I returned home, I would closely study the photos I had taken, the postcards I had chosen, and the books I bought about the sophisticated mechanisms and designs of the various Disney rides I had experienced. I got hooked on the catchy music in the Disney songs and had numerous albums with Disney songs that I sang along with and memorized. Disney also acted as a springboard for my fascination with comic books. My first comic book, probably from age six, featured Chip and Dale.

From Disney to Superheroes

From Disney characters, I quickly branched out to discover superheroes. I managed to enter comic book fandom just in time to enjoy the Silver Age of Comics and some historically great storylines, series, and new character introductions. I lost myself in the epic tales of Spider-Man, The Fantastic Four, Thor, Dr. Strange, the Silver Surfer, and the Hulk, and couldn't get enough of the Flash, Green Lantern, Plastic

Man, Metamorpho, Superman, and the Legion of Super-heroes. These amazing publications drew me into their densely populated imaginary multiverses. As a kid with an "overactive imagination" (or so I was told), it was no surprise that I always wanted to know more about the characters. Nowhere was this curiosity sated more than with superhero origin issues and stories. If I learned how *they* became superheroes, my child mind reasoned, maybe *I* could do it, too. Those cravings for information drew me to purchase, read, and re-read books like *Origins of Marvel Comics* (Lee, 1974) and *Son of Origins of Marvel Comics* (Lee, 1975); these were rare books about comic characters published in a time before they had become popular with mainstream audiences. Later, when I had the opportunity to meet Stan Lee at a comic convention, I had him sign both books. They both still mean a lot to me.

While their mythical heroic fantasies taught me moral lessons that added nuance to Disney tales and satisfied archetypal cravings I never knew I had, comic books' intertextual linkages drew me to a variety of science, fiction, and artistic topic webs. I have loved to draw and paint for as long as I can remember, and at a young age, I learned to draw cartoon characters like Fred Flintstone and Marvin the Martian. But the diverse and outstanding comic book artwork of creators like Jack Kirby, Steve Ditko, Frank Brunner, Gene Colan, Johnny Romita, George Perez, Dave Cockrum, and Dave Gibbons inspired and sharpened my artistic acumen. I had a copy of *The Mighty Marvel Superheroes Fun Book* (McCarron, 1976) that I used to use as a source of images to trace and copy until I could sketch them perfectly from memory. Later, I wore out the pages of Lee and Buscema's (1984) *How to Draw Comics the Marvel Way*. Eventually, my art interests as an adult would incorporate many of these figures as archetypal themes, for example, using Howard the Duck to represent the "Everyman" figure.

The Allure of Sports

As well as comic books, from a very young age, sports and media consumption has been a central part of my life. I was raised in a household that didn't limit "screen time." At the time, there was only one screen in the household: the family TV. And watching it was often a family event. During the week, when my dad would get home from work late, we would eat dinner and then settle into our couches together, unfold our TV tables, and eat dessert and snacks while we watched together for hours and hours, whether it was sitcoms like *All in the Family*, *The Jeffersons*, or *Sanford and Son*, various kinds of movies, hockey or baseball games. On weekends, I would wake up early and sate myself with a full slate of Saturday morning kids shows and cartoons that might include *H. R. Pufnstuf* (whose animist universe was the terrifying stuff of nightmares for my young self), *Wacky Races*, *Lancelot Link*, and *The Bugs Bunny/ Road Runner Hour*. As a family, we were prodigious television watchers and readers who also liked to travel, play games, and collect stuff.

My family would usually watch championship sports series and key games like the Stanley Cup, Super Bowl, and World Series. As soon as Toronto got its own baseball team, the whole family started watching the Blue Jays throughout the regular season. My mother loved baseball and would always join in when we were watching the games—when a player struck out in a crucial situation, that was still one of the only times I could regularly hear her cuss.

My grandfather, who lived in the apartment underneath my triplex unit, was a big wrestling fan. I remember walking into his apartment, filled with thick clouds smelling of cheap cigars. My grandfather would be perched on a chair, smoking, watching wrestling on a little black-and-white TV screen, a position we would find him in every Sunday for as long as I could remember. He knew everything about every character and would shout at the TV, moan in pain when his characters were defeated, and wave his fist in the air at a victory—offering me visceral lessons in the embodiment of sports fandom. My own sports fandom accelerated when the Blue Jays started playing winning ball in the late 1980s. I remember the outrage all Canadians felt when snarky sportscaster Bob Costas proclaimed the Blue Jays dead in the post-season series of 1989 against the dominant Oakland Athletics. "All things considered, Elvis has a better chance of coming back than the Blue Jays," Costas said, and we were all infuriated (although he was right, for that series, which made it worse). For me, my family, and friends, Blue Jays baseball permeated our conversations, social lives, and viewing habits for several wonderful years, watching superstars like George Bell, Jesse Barfield, Tom Henke, and Tony Fernandez play out- standing ball. I have lots of Blue Jays gear and numerous t-shirts that proudly proclaim my affiliation with the team—and no good Torontonian would be without Leafs hockey jerseys and t-shirts and track pants as well. My personal Bluye Jays fever probably peaked when they prevailed in two back-to-back World Series championships. Those 1992 and 1993 baseball seasons were my peak sports fan years and also helped me feel a bit more patriotic. I recall, how much it meant for me to hear that same sportscaster, Bob Costas state that, "For the first time in history, the World Championship banner will fly north of the border." Like the win when the Toronto Raptors, led by Kawhi Leonard, won the NBA Championship 2019, you never forget your home town or home country's first big championship. However, it was arguably even better for the Blue Jays the following year when Joe Carter hit a one-out, three-run walk-off home run to beat Phillie. And, like every true Blue Jays fan, I am unshakeable in my belief that, had there not been a baseball strike in 1994, we would have enjoyed that rarest of sports fan pleasures, a threepeat.

I have had the thrill of experiencing some iconic baseball games live, including a World Series game and the unforgettable 2015 game where Jose Bautista's "bat flip" marked a go-ahead run, etching itself into baseball history. When we moved to Chicago, we took up the mantle of Chicago Cubs fans and suffered through many disappointing (and also thrilling) seasons before finally savoring the sweetness of a championship. I think the family's love of sports was continued and accelerated by my children, who also extended their sports fandom into playing baseball and closely following professional and NCAA basketball, college, and USC Trojan NCAA football. They drew me into baseball spectatorship, but also national and college football, and basketball sports fandoms. Today, my sons are far bigger sports fans than I am.

Through my children, I not only expanded my love of sports but also experienced, in real-time, the wondrous world of Harry Potter. I began reading those books when my oldest son was about five. We saw the first movie on opening day, and then we saw it an additional three times. As a parent, I cherished those books and the films. And I enjoyed watching my kids embrace reading through them (and other books), carrying on the familial love of reading. We even lined up at the Westfield Old Orchard Mall's Barnes & Noble for the book releases of the Harry Potter books in Skokie; these releases were events that piqued my interest in the links between fannish spaces, retail environments, and fandoms in ways that would later lead me to ethnographically investigate, with co-authors, the fannish emplacements of sports fans at *ESPN Zone Chicago* (Kozinets et al., 2002, 2004, Sherry et al, 2001, 2004) and avid doll consumers at *American Girl Place* (Borghini et al., 2009).

Personal Passions and Media Fandom

When I was a kid, I saved my personal passion for certain shows, like *The Flintstones*, *Gilligan's Island*, and *The Addams Family*. I had a huge kid crush on Carolyn Jones from *the Addams Family* that led me, for some reason, to tell all my friends that she was actually my aunt (getting caught in that lie lost me a lot of trust). On schoolyards and behind my house, the Planet of the Apes would spur ongoing games of catch involving captures of humans by scary soldier apes—a way both to bond with family and friends and a daytime way to deal with the nightmares that the show's images roused in me. But I was already working with media texts, fantasizing about characters, extending them into my world, playing with them and through them, psychologically working things out, and making them parts of my life. The staged scenarios and the characters from these series were also part of my subconscious world. I used to dream about them quite a lot and often those dreams were very pleasurable.

The blend of space, science, and sex appeal in *Star Trek: The Original Series* fascinated me. At first, I used to clip episode names and summaries from the TV Guide and paste them into a scrapbook so I could keep track of what I had seen. Then, as more became available, I read and saved Star Trek magazines, comic books, and early books like the James Blish-authored series. When I received a little tape recorder, I tried taping episodes and then transcribing them. I believe the only one I was able to get completed was *The Deadly Years* (Season 2, Episode 12). I was very grateful for the thoroughness of the *Star Trek Concordance* (Trimble, 1976) and the scientific world-building of the *Star Fleet Technical Manual* (Joseph, 1975), purchasing them both and studying them like they were academic references. I would also assemble and paint the AMT models of the USS Enterprise, Mr. Spock (blasting some kind of three-headed snake monster, no less), tricorder, communicators, and phaser guns. Lichtenberg, Marshak, and Winston's (1975) book *Star Trek Lives!* and Sackett's (1977) *Letters to Star Trek* introduced me to the world of Star Trek fandom. Both of David Gerrold's early behind-the-scenes books, *The World of Star Trek* (Gerrold, 1973) and *The Trouble with Tribbles* (Gerrold, 1975), fascinated me. I was learning a lot from my Star Trek fandom about science, science fiction, storytelling, and how the entertainment industry functioned. More than that, I was learning from the stories and characters that it might be okay to be intelligent and that it could be acceptable to be different and true to yourself.

After that, I began reading fanzines and wrote some letters in response to campaigns to revive the series. I eagerly followed the news of the new *Star Trek: Phase Two* series, starring the Vulcan character Xon, and then was disappointed when it didn't come to fruition. I was writing my own crude forms of fan fiction at a very young age, sharing them with no one. In those bygone days, when there were only the original 79 episodes and nothing more besides pocketbooks and fan fiction, my Star Trek fandom was broad and consequential to my life and my development as a fan-scholar .

Hitting the Books

Simultaneously, my reading branched out to embrace hard and soft science fiction by Arthur C. Clarke, Robert Heinlein, Isaac Asimov, Harlan Ellison, Theodore Sturgeon, Ursula Le Guin, John Varley, and, of course, Philip K. Dick. The familiar and spiritually sideways weirdness of Dick's well-constructed universes appealed to my tastes. *The Man in the High Castle* (Dick 1962) led me to the Tao Te Ching (Tzu, 1998) and the I Ching (Huang and Huang, 1987), and deepened my interest in Eastern spiritual philosophy; *The Three Stigmata of Palmer Eldritch* (Dick, 1964) and *UBIK* (Dick, 1969) made me want to write philosophical science fiction; reading VALIS (Dick, 1981) and then Dick's massively mystical *Exegesis* (Jackson,

Lethem, and Davis, 2011) sent ectoplasmic shockwaves through my being that ripple to this day.

I entered the fantasy genre through that popular gateway, J. R. R. Tolkien's *The Lord of the Rings* and *The Hobbit* books. The original Dune trilogy by Frank Herbert was another huge favorite of mine. As a teen, I was drawn to the messianic coming-of-age story of Paul Muad'dib, set in such a distant universe, filled with bizarre and witchy mysticism. Even though I was disappointed with the David Lynch movie after eagerly anticipating it, I eventually found some sort of closure in Denis Villeneuve's much more faithful and watchable version. Again, I learned what I could and took what I needed from these texts, including memorizing and repeating "The Litany against Fear" affirmation when I felt anxious.

> "Fear is the mind-killer.
>
> Fear is the little-death that brings total obliteration.
>
> I will face my fear.
>
> I will permit it to pass over me and through me.
>
> And when it has gone past, I will turn the inner eye to see its path.
>
> Where the fear has gone, there will be nothing. Only I will remain." (Herbert, 1965, p. 370)

To be perfectly honest, it never helped. I've found that self-talk about death and obliteration is actually not a good strategy to adopt in moments of panic. My inner experimentation with The Litany Against Fear is, however, a good example of how seriously I took my entertainment and how persistently I tried to stitch my learnings from it into my thoughts, emotions, and daily experiences. The serious play involvement in media was a marker of my fannishness for as long as I can remember. When I heard intriguing ideas, I wanted to know more so I could decide whether and how to embed them into my own thinking. When I saw beautiful illustrations, I wanted to draw them. When I heard rousing music, I wanted to learn to play it.

Materializing My Restless Fandom

I was never content merely to sit back; I wanted to participate. Even today, I usually sit in front of the television with a tablet open on my lap so I can look up things and jot other things down while I watch. Even when I am supposedly audiencing, I'm a restless viewer. At first, I played, bought comic books, kept scrapbooks, and hung posters. Then I drew, wrote letters, played music, and built things. Always, there was expanding and expansionary activity in my fandom.

As I've already noted, I was a good consumer. Eventually, my consumer-driven fandom easily transitioned into economic value creation. This was because my father was a serial entrepreneur who enjoyed mixing a bit of business with pleasure. He had initially been taking me to science fiction and Star Trek conventions because I had shown such a strong interest and enthusiasm. But once he saw the action in the dealer's room, our interests changed. He started a side hustle that involved buying and selling action figures and comic books. Boxes and boxes of comic books. With my knowledge added to the financial backing of my father, "our" (really, my) collection grew rapidly. Then, we went to shows and sold most of it off. I have great memories of those few years we spent servicing fandoms from dealer's tables.

I saw *Star Wars* (that is, the original Star Wars movie) the day it came out and instantly found a new fascination that sparked my imagination. I remember coasting down a big hill on my bicycle right after seeing the movie in an afternoon matinée and fantasizing about shooting at the Death Star's exhaust port. The mystical idea of "the Force" and the movie's spiritualist leanings powerfully resonated with me and sparked my interest. And the music! I immediately bought the soundtrack album and played it over and over again, alongside the more light-hearted (and still earwormy) Meco 45" adaptation. Trying to immerse myself in that far, far away world in a time long ago, well before the Disney corporation had created Batuu and *Galaxy's Edge*, I dove into George Lucas's (1977) official paperback novel adaptation of the movie script. Seeking photos and background knowledge about the film and its world, I also collected magazines about *Star Wars*, constructed and painted models of Tie Fighters, X-Wings, and droids, did puzzles, played board games, and read Star Wars comic books. While I waited anxiously for *The Empire Strikes Back* (which did not disappoint!) and *Return of the Jedi* (which did), my Star Wars fandom freely extended into collections and collectibles, many of which I still own and cherish.

My allowance money wasn't spent on candies. It went first to books, magazines, and comics, then to albums, tickets to sports events and concerts, and music equipment. So, my passion for pop culture wasn't just limited to films and science; it also embraced the world of toys, apparel, and collectibles. Long before mainstream commercialization took over, well before being a fan was something to be proud of, I was sporting nifty Star Wars and Marvel t-shirts, often having to either order them from the inner pages of my beloved comic books or scour niche shopfront stores where decals were chosen from a wall and heat-pressed onto shirts by store staff. In the days long before eBay and Etsy, those were glorious, hard-to-come-by shirts; they were products of my fannish labors of love. And I suppose it was the natural way my fascination with media extended into material culture that may have led me to study marketing and pursue business degrees in it.

Fandom in My Teens

Let's pick up the story as I leave the innocent fannish pleasures of childhood behind and enter my teen years. Comic books and science fiction probably spurred my lasting delight in the weird and wonderful sides of pop culture. Science fiction authors like Philip K. Dick, Robert Heinlein, and Frank Herbert had fed my curiosity about mysticism, spirituality, and psychedelia. Those interests intensified and bloomed as I dove into the world of music and followed its many intertextual pathways. The Beatles' *Blue Album* was like an initiation that my friends and I shared. The Beatles made tangible and immediate my fascination with Hinduism, meditation, and mystical / psychedelic experiences. I interpreted the lyrics of songs like John Lennon's *Across the Universe* as signposts that would guide me into the positive experiential worlds of Eastern mysticism.

> "Sounds of laughter, shades of life are ringing
>
> Through my open ears, inciting and inviting me.
>
> Limitless undying love, which shines around me like a million suns,
>
> It calls me on and on, across the universe."

These were magical mental pathways that I had earlier begun exploring in books. Music intensified and directed those journeys. After *Hot Rocks* by the Rolling Stones, I went further into blues and rock and roll music, psychedelia, and psychedelic rock, including anything by Pink Floyd. Especially Pink Floyd. From Floyd and Supertramp, I noted inspiring messages that it was okay to be different and to have my own ideas and tastes. As a curious, self-conscious, and intellectual teenager, it was a relief to know that others were ostracized for being different from their peers. I've always liked the following ironic and iconic lines from Roger Hodgson's / Supertramp's *The Logical Song*, a song based on his experiences as a youth growing up in a British boarding school.

> "I said, now, watch what you say, they'll be calling you a radical
>
> A liberal, oh, fanatical, criminal
>
> Oh, won't you sign up your name? We'd like to feel you're acceptable
>
> Respectable, oh, presentable, a vegetable."

My musical tastes in those days ran from the blues of B. B. King and Muddy Waters to folk music like Cat Stevens and Bruck Cockburn, dance and electronica with the B-52s, David Bowie, and Falco, rock with Rush, The Who, Deep Purple, Rainbow, Kansas, Bad Company, The Cars, The Police, and Van Halen, and jazz with Al Di Meola, Dixie Dregs, Michael Hedges, and John McLaughlin, peppered with lots of soundtrack music. This wide blend of musical tastes, twisting in, around, and across my promiscuous appetite for various forms of media content, not only shaped my tastes but also laid the groundwork for my later academic and professional pursuits in media studies.

I remember hearing *Led Zeppelin II* for the first time. It burst forth from the amped-up car speakers of my friend Steve's golden 1972 Ford Mustang convertible as we zoomed in a packed car down the highway. That music, like the songs of The Beatles and The Rolling Stones, was life-changing, and its discovery coincided with a range of other important changes in my life. But it wasn't enough for me simply to listen to the songs, read album liner notes and lyrics, or discuss them with friends. I wanted to know more about the musicians, the instruments, and the songs. I wanted to hear the stories behind them. So I bought and read magazines about the musicians and bands I was into, and I read biographies of legendary rock gods like Jim Morrison and Jimi Hendrix.

And Led Zeppelin. I'd like to draw upon the words of the talented cultural critic and author Erik Davis, who wrote about his passion for the band as follows:

> "Led Zeppelin, with great cunning and an elemental command of "light and shade," crafted records into mythic enchantments. . . As you can probably tell, I write as one thoroughly enchanted. As with many boys (and some girls) growing up in the long fade of classic rock culture, Led Zeppelin offered me more than a soundtrack for getting loaded and making out. Listening and loving the band was also a rite of passage, a guided tour through an internal landscape that was changing as dramatically as the body and the loins and the world were changing... And no one offered a better song cycle for my escape into shadow than Led Zeppelin. In his delirious potboiler *Hammer of the Gods*, Stephen Davis [Davis, 1985] called the band "a mystery cult with several million initiates." It's more than a metaphor: Zeppelin offered fans a peculiarly powerful mytho-poetic identification beyond the boundaries of the music itself. As Andy Fyfe [2003, p. 14] writes, "*Led Zep IV* plus *The Lord of the Rings* plus discovering girls and booze equals Very Powerful Teenage Male Experience." Sure, it was cock rock, but it was also a mystery, wrapped in an enigma, stuffed into a cock. Zep's theatrical soundscapes, cool covers, and scattered allusions to *the Lord of the Rings* served as a secret wink, an affirmation that between the cracks of what I already suspected was going to turn out to be a rather disenchanted world nestled some resplendent other [reality]." (Davis, 2005, pp. 6-8)

My experiences were not dissimilar. Led Zeppelin taught me that it was all right to explore some of the darker sides of my mystical passions and fascinations. As with many fans, my intertextual readings of Led Zeppelin led me to Aleister Crowley's work and the Temple of the Golden Dawn, and those works led me to Tarot cards, black candles, and scary t-shirts. With my best friend, I began undertaking weekly pilgrimages to watch the Jimi Hendrix and Led Zeppelin movie double feature at Toronto's Music Hall—a personally significant ritual I will recount in more detail in another book in this series, which frames **Fandom as Devotion**. And my collection of concert stubs speaks volumes about my many live music adventures. Those little scraps of paper capture powerful memories from performances by some historically great bands and musicians. I still love live music today and catch concerts when possible.

That was the time and the music that inspired me to begin composing music, start jamming with a band, and play the occasional venue. That music combined with that thing inside me that wanted to always know more. To learn how the sausage was made and maybe to try to make some of my own. I had seriously considered pursuing my dream of being an artist and applying to the Ontario College of Arts. But, instead, my passion for music was translated into a desire to manage my own band and understand the music business. And that hunger for understanding led me to business school, an MBA, and, of all things, the world of financial consulting.

CHAPTER 2:

Rob: Mixing Business with Pleasure

Entering the Ph.D. Program

I didn't enter the Ph.D. program intending to study music or fandom, though. When I entered the program at Queen's University in Kingston, Ontario, a university town that is situated about halfway between Toronto and Montreal, I actually thought I would be working in organizational psychometrics, or the construction and statistical testing of new psychology scales for business uses like recruitment. But, along the way, I found my way. John Dowling, one of the founders of organizational behavior's institutional theory, introduced me to ethnography and phenomenology in his challenging and wacky class, which often ended with him sharing and mostly drinking a box of wine and telling tales of his various academic exploits.

I probably felt most seen, however, when I took Steve Arnold's Marketing Philosophy class. Wearing big round glasses, with white hair cut into a bowl style, Steve was an athletic guy, a runner and a roller blader. He brought a combination of being disciplined, methodical, precise, approachable, and enthusiastic to his pedagogy—a unique and appropriate combination. In his class, he uses the lens of marketing as a science to take apart the entire procedure for doing research and understanding the world. He armed his students with numerous readings and insights about the philosophical underpinnings of knowledge—our ontologies, epistemologies, axiologies, and practices—and those elements helped us construct very rigorously grounded views of research and method.

Steve introduced us to the work of another Stephen, Stephen J. Gould. This was not the evolutionary theorist, but a consumer researcher who emphasized the value of introspection in research and was subsequently excoriated for it from across the field. His examples, which drew from his own charting of various bodily energies and how his consumption affected them, were intensely personal. Many of the stuffy academics at the time (and probably still today) found it uncomfortable to read about a researcher contemplating his own sexual arousal, spirituality, and altered states of consciousness and evaluating how food, stimulants, and meditation affects them. Yet I found his work fascinating; he became an early academic role model for his courage, openly spiritual stance, and honesty. Looking back at this intriguing work, which argued for the value of penetrant personal introspection as well as attention to the regulation of flows of energy through our bodies and minds, I also find intriguing clues about the role of entertainment and media in the process. Consider the following passage:

> "When I feel energized and want to get more absorbed and excited, I might read about a shamanistic experience or watch a television show or movie about one to "get off" and invoke potential energies. Thus, I love to watch shows on the Discovery Channel about aboriginal peoples and their spiritual rituals because they tend to arouse in me the impulse to jump up and down in ecstasy, similar to my experience with alcohol. Sometimes I may actually do some empathetic crazy dancing, but, more often, I

channel the energy by letting it move from my arms and legs, which feel like jumping and dancing, to my heart and head in a way that is ironically still and calm in the midst of the show's excitement." (Gould 1991, p. 204)

Gould's exploration of his use of certain media to incite his energetic passions resonates with our definition of fandoms as vibrant cultures of passionate engagement. In this book series, we will be developing ideas related to the notion that powerful passions are central to contemporary fandoms. Our book, **Fandom as Desire,** explores the way our biological, emotional, and even spiritual passions permeate our relationships with consumer culture and fandom. Maintaining this perspective and exploring it will draw our attention to the ways that fandom expresses some of our innermost passions, embodying pleasures and wants, and touching on the need for social change and longing for utopia.

Sacred Consumer Experiences

I remember one class where my favorite professor, Steve Arnold, brought in a copy of a very theoretical academic paper for us to look at, with the reviews from the journal it was submitted to. The paper ended up being from his now-classic work, co-written with my good friend and colleague, Eileen Fischer (also a former student of Steve's), applying philosophical hermeneutics to consumer and marketing research. Following is a quote.

"The [pre-]understanding of consumer researchers is found in two interrelated traditions —experience as a consumer and experience as a researcher. If we, for instance, knew nothing of shopping in modern stores with complex arrays of merchandise, of the artistry and imagination that inform advertising, or of the complex emotions associated with gift giving, we could not begin to make sense of the many phenomena we study. Philosophical hermeneutics counsels us to capitalize more fully on [pre-]understanding rather than trying to put it aside when we take up our research" (Arnold and Fischer, 1994, p. 57).

So much of that short paragraph has worked its way into my own work over the years. When I teach classes about consumer behavior, I always ask students to keep in mind their identities as consumers first. Only secondarily should they think of themselves as marketers. In my research, the notion of pre-understanding and subjective knowledge is at the very core of ethnographic understanding, baked into the principles of immersion, engagement, and participation that have played such a big role in my development of netnography. This very section, autobiographical and introspective, is a testament to the lasting impact that this work on reflective hermeneutics had on me.

There were some readings in the *Marketing Theory* classes that absolutely floored me when I first encountered them. One of those was called "The Sacred and the Profane in Consumer Behavior: Theodicy on the Odyssey" by Russell Belk, Melanie Wallendorf, and John F. Sherry, Jr. That article was the result of the Consumer Behavior Odyssey I discussed above. The Odyssey was a summerlong ethnographic field trip across the United States in an RV that resulted in some of the most influential scholarship in the field of marketing. Acting as anthropologists of consumer behaviors traveling far and wide to see the reality of lived, everyday consumers, that article brilliantly located Mircea Eliade's categories of the sacred and profane in contemporary American consumer culture. The authors defined the sacred as distinct from the religious and provided a blueprint for exploring the mythological, archetypal, and spiritual experiences present throughout the marketplace realm of consumption.

"For many contemporary consumers, there are also elements of life with no connection to formal religion that are nonetheless revered, feared, and treated with the utmost respect. Examples include flags, sports stars, national parks, art, automobiles, museums, and collections. Whether we call the reverence for these things religious, contemporary consumers treat them as set apart, extraordinary, or sacred, just as elements of nature are sacred in naturistic religions and certain icons are sacred to followers of contemporary, organized religions. Although the specific focal objects differ, the same deeply moving, self-transcending feelings may attend each, and the same revulsion may occur when these objects are not treated with respect. Religion is one, but not the only, context in which the concept of the sacred is operant."
—Belk, Wallendorf, and Sherry (1989), p. 57

Coming to the Ph.D. program with my life history as a fan, I couldn't help but interpret what I was learning through the lenses of my fandoms. If sports stars, art, museums, and collections were viewed as sacred and set apart from the mundane, then maybe comic books, hard rock, and media science fiction could be, too. The **Fandom as Devotion** book in this series is a mature extension that grew from this early fascination, benefiting from the many conversations about it that Henry and I shared over the decades.

Mind you, I had only very rudimentary forms of those ideas in mind as I studied for my doctorate. Once I had passed my comprehensive exams (in both Organizational Behavior and Marketing), I was ready to think about doing a dissertation that brought all these ideas together. Over a couple of beers in the Grad Club and with a couple of well-chosen arguments, Steve convinced me to abandon my pursuit of a psychological testing dissertation and join the dark side: marketing. After throwing a few ideas out, we finally came to one we both loved, which was to research Star Trek fans through the eyes of a consumer researcher.

A Dissertation on Star Trek Fandom

As a long-time Star Trek fan who had waited decades for the series' return, I was eagerly following the new seasons of "Star Trek: The Next Generation" (TNG) while I was at school. At that time, TNG was not just a popular television show; it was a cultural phenomenon, shattering all precedents in syndicated television records. One poll at the time found that more than half of all Americans regarded themselves to be Star Trek fans, making Trekdom a majority culture in the United States.

I pitched the idea of embarking on an ethnographic journey using the lenses of marketing and consumer research to understand the longevity, depth, and communal connection of Star Trek fandom. I conceived of this venture as "(re-)joining the tribe" of other Star Trek fans, a term I used both in my own reflections and in explanations to others. This phrase encapsulated my intention to not just observe but to continue to actively participate in the fan community. I planned to attend conventions, and partake in other fan gatherings, immersing myself in the rituals and cultural practices of the group.

Steve loved the idea. And so, back to the world of fandom I went.

At this time, the Queen's University library, where I spent a lot of time studying, had just installed a bunch of terminals. They were all now equipped with a newfangled thing called "Netscape," a new browser for the World Wide Web. I had been using a home computer since the mid-1980s, and was well-acquainted with CompuServe and other services, but this new computer revolution came at exactly the right time for me. I started spending my time on those computers, looking up everything, and finding a massive world of Star Trek fandom with thousands of websites and discussion boards already going strong.

I went to a few local Star Trek conventions and, from there, joined a nearby Star Trek fan club. In **Locations of Fandom**, I write more about my ethnography and what I found but suffice it to say that I was spending a lot of my dissertation research time doing what fans do, with other fans, reading about fandom, and thinking about it. It was during this time that I discovered the works of a number of Star Trek and fan scholars, including Camille Bacon-Smith, Lisa Lewis, and John Fiske. And, of course, Henry Jenkins, whose *Textual Poachers* had just been published a few years before.

It seemed to me at the time (and it still does), that the timing for a dissertation that looks at the technological side of fandom was just right, and I just happened to be in a great position to explore these ideas. Sitting at the very cusp of that digital age as I undertook my dissertation research, I subscribed to a web account from Cyberlink Online and started teaching myself how to program in HTML. I used these new skills to create a website dedicated to my research called "To Boldly Go: The Star Trek Research Web page." I described the site as the homepage of "a lifelong Star Trek fan who is now pursuing PhD research into the Star Trek culture and other media fan cultures (such as the X-Files) and what they tell us about consumer behavior in the contemporary or postmodern age." The site contained numerous links to other fan sites, my PhD proposal and early findings, information about postmodernism and consumer research, some original summaries, and information about other scholarly investigations of Star Trek culture and also presented visitors with a chance to add their own input to my investigation by answering a series of questions about their relationship to Star Trek fandom grouped under 14 headings with names like collections, types of goods, communicating about goods, Treknology, and Trek activism.

That web page ended up yielding online fan interviews, some lasting almost 2 years of back-and-forth email conversation, with 65 fans from 12 different countries.

As well, the page yielded the following email from one "Cyberman@MIT.EDU" address.

"Hi. I stumbled across your webpage doing a routine surf of the net and was flattered to see your attentive treatment of my work. I would be delighted to know more about you and your project and would be happy to be a sounding board for your ideas as they develop."

It was signed Henry Jenkins. My heart skipped a beat when I read it. Henry Jenkins, whose work on fans I was already a big fan of. The next day, I spoke to my thesis supervisor and asked him if we could invite Henry to be a member of my dissertation committee. He thought it was a great idea.

The connection had been made. At the time, I had no idea how substantial and long-lasting it would become.

Melding Consumer and Fan Research

From the get-go, Henry proved to be a patient and brilliant mentor. I learned immeasurably from his comments and suggestions and incorporated them into my ethnography of Star Trek fandom. That work, which transpired over 20 months of fieldwork at conventions, fan club meetings, and online, was eventually published in the *Journal of Consumer Research. JCR,* as it is commonly called, is the leading journal in the sub-field of marketing that looks at consumers from a range of disciplinary perspectives, such as psychology, sociology, and anthropology. When I entered the field, consumer research had just begun considering the collective elements of consumer behavior by including things such as subcultures and forms of consumption that seemed set apart or sacred.

Although consumer researchers Beth Hirschman and Morris Holbrook had looked into entertainment consumption, their research was mainly composed of individual reflections or overviews without ethnographic or phenomenological data. The field had not yet noticed that fandom was a significant phenomenon that might inform our greater understanding of contemporary consumers and consumer culture. In my ethnography of Star Trek fandom, I sought to correct that. In that study, I laid out a vision for a view of consumer culture research that would study the more passionate, collective, and participatory forms of consumption that I was seeing in media fandom, first, but also in a range of other activities. I began by linking together the concept of "fans" with that of "consumers."

"Fans are devoted, loyal consumers who invest more of themselves in their consumption and, therefore, who expect more from it. Very similar processes may drive consumer involvement, interest, affinities, belief in, and loyalty to particular products or forms of consumption. Consumer researchers should consider studying the situated cultural and subcultural articulations that underlie the new product marketer's Holy Grail of a cult product such as 3Com's Palm Pilot, the Apple iMac, the Polaroid iZone, the Volkswagen Beetle, Ural motorcycles, the National Association for Stock Car Auto Racing (NASCAR), or the Entertainment and Sports Programming Network (ESPN). This article suggests that researchers look for stigmatic boundaries (that enhance internal community), subcultural sanctuary (that sponsors loyalty), fantasy-oriented imagery (that engages the imagination), moral utopian and mythic dimensions (that provide ideological legitimation and help build the possible self), and amelioration of the taint of commercialized cultural exploitation." (Kozinets 2001, p. 85).

Almost all of my research examining consumers and consumer culture drew its inspiration from this framing of consumers as motivated by passion and becoming increasingly collective and participatory in their orientation. For example, my work on consumer activism initially examined online activist groups and compared their moral compass and participatory nature with fannish groups (Kozinets and Handelman, 1998; Kozinets and Handelman, 2004).

As I began researching online consumers and finding ways that they created participatory cultures around their consumption interests, these associations to fandom and its study were never far from my mind. In the article in which I introduced "netnography," which has grown to become a recognized way to conduct qualitative research on digital experiences, I studied coffee enthusiasts. My experiences with fan groups definitely colored the way I approached this study. For example, consider the collective consumption enthusiasm among coffee aficionados, which I wrote about in a 2002 article introducing the netnography method:

> "The previous comments, in which a coffeephile ascribes his increasing investment to the influence of a fellow newsgroup member, suggest the power of the newsgroup to acculturate consumption practices. This acculturating force, which drives increasing investments in a new cultural interest. . . is often mapped out in coffeephile communications, tracing a gustatory route through, for example, cappuccino, macchiato, and con pannas to espresso. In total, this set of united products can be

interpreted as a "product constellation" (Solomon and Assael 1987) that . . . might be thought of as a particular consumption web that increasingly draws a group of consumers into deeper and more profound levels of (sub) cultural involvement and enthusiasm, consumption, and investment." (Kozinets 2002, p. 68).

The idea of a "consumption web" in which members of a culture drew one another further into different types of interconnected consumption and social behaviors originated in my ethnographic work among Star Trek and other fans. The consumption web concept, in fact, was an entire chapter in my dissertation work and originally illustrated how different types of Star Trek fans become educated about and drawn into various specific consumption paths that laid out their fandom but also left room for their own agentic interpretations and creativity.

With Stephen Brown and John Sherry, I would conduct a series of netnographies to investigate retro-brands, which we defined as "relaunched historical brands with updated features" (Brown, Kozinets, and Sherry, 2003b, p. 19). In that study, I chose to include online Star Wars fans so that I could incorporate more fandom research perspectives. Furthermore, I included a breakfast cereal fandom for a product, Quisp, that included cartoon advertising created by fan favorite animator Jay Ward. Ward had created the popular *Bullwinkle and Rocky* cartoon (that research site was eventually cut and appears in Brown, Kozinets, and Sherry, 2003a). Our interpretations of behavior of Volkswagen Beetle enthusiasts, which constituted our final research field, explicitly linked their behavior with participatory culture and fannish behaviors.

Later, I would edit a book called *Consumer Tribes* with Bernard Cova and Avi Shankar which would further knit together the study of fandoms and consumer collectives. The book contained chapters by various authors merging studies of Tom Petty fans (Schau and Muñiz, 2007), fans of the British Royal Family (Otnes and Malaran, 2007), car enthusiasts and "cruisers" (Brownlie, Hewer, and Treanor, 2007), Hummer fans (Luedicke and Giesler, 2007), Harry Potter fandom (Brown, 2007), Warhammer gamers (Park, Deshpande, Cova, and Pace, 2007), fetish fans (Langer, 2007), and many others. All were viewed through the lens of consumer tribes as both consumers and members of unique participatory cultures. I wrote a chapter returning to my work on Star Trek, expanding it to consider the impacts of digital technologies on the growth of its fandoms (Kozinets, 2007).

Throughout my career and to the present day, I have been thinking and writing about the various ways in which fandoms and consumer collectives interrelate and overlap and what we can learn from this about market mediation, marketing, and consumer culture. My conversations with Henry for *Convergence Culture*, and later for *Spreadable Media*, helped develop these ideas.

For a volume on the digital transformation of business, I decided to directly tackle these intersections by looking at "brand fans" and considering what happens when entertainment and marketing intersect with participatory culture and the community-building affordances of digital technologies online (Kozinets, 2010). For Denise Mann's *WiredTV* volume, I wrote a chapter that peered critically into business's increasing appropriation of the term "fan" to discuss their customers. Analogizing with product designers' notion of "feature creep," in which product designers keep adding features to a product and end up complicating it, I called the phenomenon "fan creep" (Kozinets, 2014). It seemed to me that marketers were unnecessarily and unhelpfully using the idea of fandom to muddy the waters about just how enthusiastic, collective, or participatory their customers might be.

As streams of thought, these ideas thread throughout my theorizing. Through it all, my foundational experiences as a fan, a consumer, and a researcher, and my life orientation as a fan and a consumer researcher, have guided me to topics and methods that seemed appropriate and true to understanding these fascinating interfaces of popular and mass culture, playing themselves out in the expanding worlds of consumer and digital culture. Mind-melding the worlds of consumer culture research and studies of fandom continues to fascinate me. Those efforts culminate in these volumes.

CHAPTER 3:

Henry: Performing as a Fan

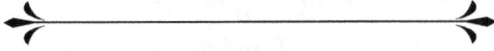

Henry here. Like Rob, I became a fan at an early age. My first fandom was Batman 66 – the first series I can recall watching regularly and intentionally. I would have been eight years old when it debuted. But I did not simply watch the series; I also acted it out in my backyard with the neighborhood kids. My mother made me a cowl and a batarang to add some vividness to the process. I had a tree house where the kids would gather, read comics, and plot new adventures. We owned a recording of the *Batman* theme song and I would jump on the bed with my brother in our best Bang! Bam! Pow! fashion. I was young, but my experiences with Batman represented a passionate and committed relationship with a television series that was social (at least in terms of the neighborhood gang and the scale of my world at the time) and creative (in so many ways!). From the start, it was less about collecting commercial products (though I did plenty of this) but more about using the media content as a jumping off place (literally and figuratively) for trying on identities and transforming the world around me (Jenkins, 2007).

Spooky Stuff

The same kids made the transition with me from *Batman* to *Famous Monsters of Filmland* and the vintage horror movies it celebrated (Jenkins, 2012). I transitioned fairly seamlessly from the Green Lantern (we took Batman into an extended DC universe) to Dracula, even using the same ring to hypnotize my prey or to produce material manifestations of my power. A special issue of *Famous Monsters* taught us how to do monster makeup and I used to spend hours in front of the mirror with grease paint, crepe hair, lipstick, and mascara trying to perfect different monsters. I had fantasies of rivaling Lon Chaney, Man of a Thousand Faces, when I grew up (ignoring the fact that nobody was making silent movies anymore).

My father and I would sit up past my bedtime as we assembled and painted all of the original Aurora monster models. I passed them along to my son, who shared my passion for "all things spooky" (being a Haunted Mansion nerd). Today, Dracula and Wolfman, two of my favorites, sit on my desk in the office. I had brought them in as stage dressing for my appearance in a documentary about the cult film, *Monster Squad*.

At the peak of my monster madness, I begged my parents for a Super 8 movie camera and in the meantime, I was writing monster movie scenarios and roping my friends into signing contracts with me to act "exclusively" in my movies. I found one of the contracts a few years back. My mother had stored it in the attic; it was written on the cardboard backing from a dress shirt.

How I Caught the Movie Bug

Famous Monsters started my obsession with older movies. It entered a new phase when a local Atlanta television station produced *Tubby and Lester*, a local children's program where the hosts imitated Laurel and Hardy and showed old Hal Roach and Mack Sennett comedies instead of cartoons. I had my birthday party on the show and I still cherish the plastic bowler that I was gifted on the show as having been the birthday boy. My best friend Mike, my brother Russell and I dressed up as the Keystone Cops for Halloween.

Eventually, I <u>did</u> get a camera and editing equipment and made a number of Super 8 films. I so identified with *The Fableman*'s representation of amateur filmmaking. I came along a bit later and with fewer resources and less commitment, but damn, we did love to make movies!

By the time I got my camera, my tastes had shifted towards *Mad* magazine and its movie parodies. Their spirit pervades my short films. There are still dozens of important films from the 60s and 70s which I know only through *Mad*'s satires, which exposed me to many worlds that my mother would not have let me visit directly at that age, But the persistence of classic Hollywood runs through my amateur films as well. *The Secret Life of Walter Mitty Jr.* – my take on the classic Thurber story – was about a high school student whose daydreams I constructed by inserting scenes from Errol Flynn movies so that racing to the bus becomes *The Charge of the Light Brigade*. I wrote my seventh-grade term paper – an opus of maybe ten pages – on the history of American cinema. My father always joked that I have been rewriting and expanding it ever since.

When I was 12 or 13, I was helping my mother clear out her family homestead in Midtown Atlanta, going through a dusty attic when we stumbled upon an old trunk. Its contents would change my life. Inside were dozens of old magazines from the World War II era – mostly news magazines but a wide arrange of other genres. I spent hours reading them, finding patterns, and seeing the connections between news and cultural events of the 1940s. At that same time, I discovered a local station that played only vintage radio shows, and I quickly started to see similar patterns and connections there. This mode of analysis would blossom during my undergraduate days when I reviewed films for the *Georgia State Signal* and would motivate me to go to graduate school. It was a passion and an intellectual interest but not yet a fandom because I was going this path alone. But it led me to deepen my involvement with old movies, initiated by *Famous Monsters*, and to go deeper into the world of movie buffs.

I fed my love of classic Hollywood cinema with dozens of movie buff coffee table books (still on the shelves of my office) and with Leonard Maltin's guidebooks. My friend Edward and I would review the index and check which films we saw. I still keep lists today. I have seen more than 365 films in 2024 by the end of the summer and am still going strong. I attend Cinecon, The San Francisco Silent Film Festival, the Los Angeles Noir Alley Festival, and many others each year. I am frankly obsessive about Turner Classic Movies, which reminds me anew each day of why I love old films and why I went to graduate school to study cinema history. Edward and I get together to see old and new movies whenever I am in Atlanta.

Growing up when and where I did, I was also exposed to some pretty noxious representations of race and gender. I recall watching *Song of the South* with my grandmother in Atlanta's Fox Theater. It was the first film I had ever seen which represented my home state (*Gone with the Wind* was in my future). Afterwards, my grandmother showed me the back of the theater where there was a walled off area where Black patrons were required to sit. It was a powerful experience. I loved the film – there are things in it that still speak to me even if maturity, historical knowledge, and racial awareness have taught me to question much that is on the screen there.

Something similar happened to me with representations of Asia. The *Jungle Book* was the first Disney film I saw and I thought it was amazing. I read all of Sax Rohmer's Fu Manchu novels, which spoke of adventures in exotic places, wild animals, strange scents, secret passages, trap doors, and deadly poisons, which stirred my heart as a young boy. Both of them were full of stereotypes of Indians in loincloths and the "yellow peril." But they also brought me to visit India and China as an adult because they exposed me to a sense of wonder about other parts of the world. And I learned for myself, firsthand, what these cultures were really about.

Fandom: You're Soaking in It

Performing and cosplay (well before the term was coined) were central to my childhood. When we watched something in my neighborhood, we often found ways to embody it and, in the process, reimagine it, making our own stories that built on the elements we liked best. We didn't yet have action figures to play with when I was a boy, though I did recognize so much of myself watching my son play with his *He-Man Masters of the Universe* toys in the 1980s. We did have Soakies, a kind of bubble bath which came in plastic versions of cartoon characters, A family photograph shows that I was into remix practices even as a kid, I have unscrewed and swapped the heads on several characters, and the nature of the Soakie was that you had one or two characters from each series so crossover stories were the only way to go.

Figure 2: Henry with Soakies Figures

Like Rob, my fandom was fostered by nurturing family members, each of whom, in their own way, were fans. I recall seeing my grandmother pound on the coffee table with her bedroom slippers as she got wrapped up in a televised wrestling match, but she also introduced me to the pleasures of silent movies – especially the clowns. My father loved the *Pogo* comic strip, and I have my mother's drawing of its lead character, which used to hang on his wall as a student at Georgia Tech and is now framed and hanging on the wall of my office at USC. He also loved science fiction—*Star Trek* in particular—and the first time I saw an episode ("Shore Leave") was sneaking into the living room after my bedtime to see what my parents were watching. My mother loved all things Disney and this soon became the cultural currency that glued my family together. It still is since my brother, my sister-in-law, and subsequent members of their dynasty all love Disney, and it remains a great conversation starter when the Jenkins clans get together. My cousin George Jr. was part of the Atlanta fan scene as a fan artist and convention organizer, and he became a role model for what engaging in fandom might mean to me.

When I met the woman who would become my wife, she was my initial guide into the world of fan fiction. We raised a son who has become a fan in his own right and has drawn me into so many fan texts, most importantly for this book being ASMR. When I solicit autobiographies from students in my fandom classes, they almost inevitably share how their family relations shape their entry into this world, a topic I or someone else really should tackle more fully someday.

I have thought often about a moment which changed how I understood fandom. Rob's account of his reading of nonfiction books about the "*Making of Star Trek*" or the design of Disney World rides feels very familiar to me from my own adolescence. I admired the people who made the things I liked and wanted to know more about what was happening behind the scenes. Some (Obsession Inc.,

2009) have called this affirmational fandom, and it is often seen as characteristic of how men consume media. I took this approach as definitive of what it meant to be a fan.

When I met Cynthia, I saw something different. We were both interested in the classic Star Trek episode "The Menagerie,'" which added a frame story to the original series pilot. The core of the episode centered on an almost totally different crew. Leonard Nimoy's Spock was a holdover, but his personality was rethought:Spock displays strong emotions, lacking the stoicism and rationality that would define later understanding of Vulcan culture. I understood all of this through my knowledge of the production process; Cynthia approached it from within the storyworld. We had seen Spock experiment by trying to rid himself of all emotions and become a purely rational being. But Spock was a mixed-race man whose mother had been human and so it made sense that he might have other phases in his life when he experimented with those aspects of his identity. "Menagerie" just captured a moment where Spock was trying to be more human, which he understood as being more emotional.

Cynthia was a transformational fan, according to more contemporary formulations, and indeed many women, queer fans, and fans of color are transformational fans because the series was not written for them and so they become adept at operating within the fictional world to restory elements that do not fully satisfy them.

How I Became a Klingon (More than Once)

From the start, television was not simply something I watched but a springboard for other activities. Watching *Star Trek* resulted in me organizing "landing parties" onto strange new worlds in the pine forests, vacant lots, and grassy yards of a suburban Atlanta that was still taking shape around us. In high school, I was cast as a Klingon commander for a theatrical staging of "Trouble with Tribbles."

Years later, I assumed the oxymoronic role of Klingon Ambassador in a mail-based role-playing game, taking great pleasure in infuriating a strait-laced guy who was my Federation counterpart who could not fully process that my taunts were part of the role-playing and wanted to have me thrown out of the game for poor sportsmanship.

And years later still, after I was already established as a fandom studies scholar, J.J. Abrams invited me to be an extra on his Star Trek cinematic reboot, and again, I was cast as a Klingon commander, so now I was a canonical Klingon, though since the sequence ended up on the cutting room floor and then as a DVD extra (in silhouette), it is unclear whether this character is part of the canon or the fanon of Star Trek. Well, I recognize myself in that murky shot, but I doubt anyone else would.

And so it goes.

Let me be clear. I don't do sports. The only sports I care about are fictional ones. I cry at *League of Their Own*. I enjoy WWE wrestling. I was a fan of *Friday Night Lights*. I once spent a warm summer afternoon watching the Austrian national quidditch team prep for the World Cup competition. I watch the Super Bowl for the ads and the halftime show.

As for music, there was a brief shining moment in my undergraduate years when I had a press pass to the Atlanta nightclubs and used it frequently at a moment when Patti Smith, The Ramones, Devo, The Police, Blondie, the B52s, The Sex Pistols, Robby Robinson, and so many other new wave and punk artists were bursting onto the stage. I sometimes brush across something I like – Neoswing, world music, and a bit of K-Pop, but it rarely gets too intense. I fear, as a founding figure in the development of fandom studies, that it may have taken shape around my biases. For that reason, I am working with Rob to bridge those divides in this book series.

What Fandom Means to Me

For me, being a fan means participating in a subculture I had belonged to most of my life. Across that time, many different media properties have sparked my passion and interests. I am a fan of television, film, comics, and books, less so of sports and music though sometimes, I get strongly attached to a particular performer – Patti Smith, may I sing your praises here! To me, fandom is a way of life, a mode of engaging with culture, and not a singular relationship to a particular media narrative. And when I bond with a performer, I bond for life. I still go back and watch Batman 66 episodes, still read Mad on occasion, and now own a CD-ROM with the full original run of *Famous Monsters*…

I am polycentric and perverse in my relation to popular culture. I fall in love with fan objects fairly easily and am motivated to share that love with others. I think beyond the ending and beyond what the work tells us explicitly about the characters and their emotional lives. For the kinds of fans I study, the character is most often the point of entry, though I am personally also drawn to richly conceived worlds. I have learned to read media through my involvement in the subculture and apply that interpretive lens to pretty much everything I watch.

I form rituals around beloved objects: My wife and I snuggled down together in a hammock to read the final Harry Potter book by flashlight when it came out at midnight and continued reading together by the dawn's early light.

Yes, I have written and published some fan fiction (*Blake 7, A Christmas Carol*) and read much more. I collect meaningful objects. I go regularly to fan conventions — large (the 150,000 attendee San Diego Comic-Con) and small (the 100 person or so Escapade). And yes, I have engaged in cosplay on more than one occasion. I was even depicted in the *Chronicle of Higher Education* holding a Batleth (a Klingon battle sword).

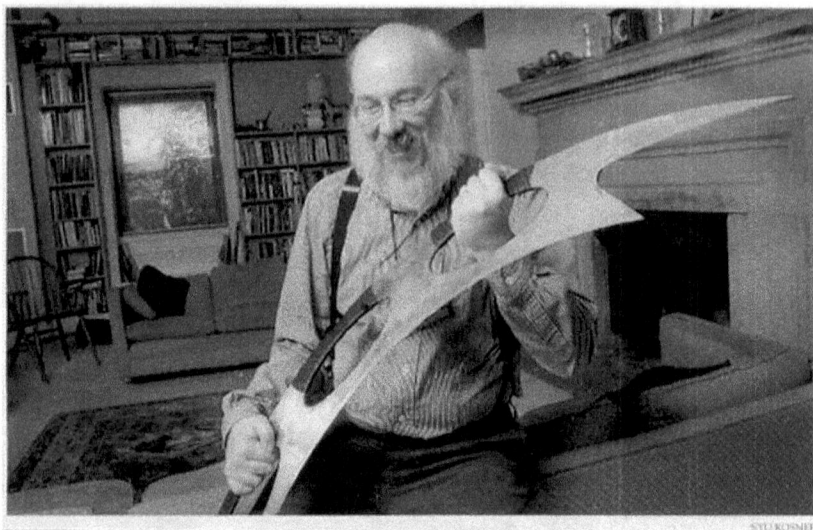

Figure 3: Henry with Bat'leth

I am and always have been a fan. People often ask me to name my guilty pleasures and the framework doesn't work for me since I do not associate pleasure with guilt. Instead, I learned to appreciate all kinds of popular culture on their own terms – whether or not they had the resources they needed to fully realize their vision. Being a fan has changed how I saw myself, the world, and ultimately, shaped who I would become professionally.

By the time I was an undergraduate, I was regularly going to the Atlanta Fantasy Fair (which would become Dragon-Con). By the time I graduated, I was reading fanzines of various kinds and actively engaged with a fan community. Being a fan had become not only a creative outlet for me, but participating within a fandom was a central part of my social identity.

CHAPTER 4:

Henry: My Life as an Aca-Fan

What John Fiske Taught Me

I went to graduate school to study American film history. While I was there, I was frustrated because the roles imagined for spectators in film theory in the 1980s were nowhere near as rich or as active or as meaningful as those I had experienced as a fan and thus rang false – more than that, elitist. I came close to dropping out due to feelings of alienation until John Fiske entered my life, a breath of fresh air, with his tanned and leathery skin, his toothy grin, and Akumbra hat. The memory of my first encounter with him -- walking across a frozen Iowa wasteland -- has become bigger than life, growing in mythic stature over time.

Fiske had been mentored by Raymond Williams, the founding figure in British cultural studies, and he brought with him the rich tradition – if you can call something then so newly minted a tradition– of Birmingham cultural studies writing on subcultures and audiences.

He taught us to start from the assumption that humans rarely engage in meaningless activities, that we are animals that make meaning out of everything in our environment and are deeply motivated by the search for meaningful lives. We researchers may not understand why someone else finds the culture they like meaningful

– it may not be meaningful to us – but our jobs as cultural scholars is to dig deeper and find out what it means to which groups in which contexts. We don't get to dismiss other people as dupes; we have to understand first and critique second.

In *Reading the Popular*, Fiske (1989) draws a direct connection between pleasure and meaning, which makes the connections to fans and fandom clear from the start:

> "Culture making (and culture is always in process, never achieved) is a social process; all meanings of self, of social relations, all the discourses and the texts that play such important cultural roles can circulate only in relation to the social system, in our case that of white, patriarchal capitalism, Any social system needs a cultural system of meanings that serve either to hold it in place or destabilize it, to make it more or less amenable to change. Culture (and its meanings and pleasures) is a constant succession of social practices; it is therefore political; it is centrally involved in the distribution and possible redistribution of various forms of social power" (p. 1)

So many of Fiske's key ideas (Jenkins 2016; Jenkins 2011) are in this brief passage – the focus on culture-making as an active and open-ended process, the linkage of pleasure and meaning, of culture and politics, of social and cultural power. And you can see how some of my ideas about fans as building their own cultural community on the basis of their conspicuous consumption and resignification of cultural materials emerge from the underlying assumptions provided by this model. Fiske always wrote from the vantage point of the consumer and citizen, never of the producer and the political powerbroker, though I have learned to speak to and with such people across my career.

Fiske opened his book, *Understanding Popular Culture* (1989), with a chapter examining the various clusters of meanings which consumers applied to blue jeans, the ways that advertisers tapped and shaped those meanings through branding, and the ways we might understand brands and consumer goods as part of the larger category of popular cultures. We might see this essay as anticipating the fusion between fandom studies and consumer culture research which is represented by **Frames of Fandom.**

Fiske encouraged me to reflect on my own experiences as a fan, inspired me to write and publish my first essay on *Star Trek* fans, commissioned my first book, *Textual Poachers: Television Fans and Participatory Culture*, and introduced me to John Tulloch, who would co-author my second, lesser-known book, *Science Fiction Audiences: Watching Star Trek and Doctor Who* (Tulloch and Jenkins, 1995). Fiske passed away in 2020, but he had retired from the field many years before. I would have only a few brief conversations with him after he retired, but I still hear his voice in my head as I write these passages.

Figure 2: Henry with John Fiske

Fiske had wanted *Textual Poachers* to provide a general introduction to fans and fandom in contemporary culture. I found I could not write such a book. There was not enough research yet. Only now, following three-plus decades of expanding waves of scholarship, could I imagine doing so, and even here, we've ended up with fourteen such books rather than one. What *Poachers* did was to dig deep into the mostly female fan fiction-writing community as a way of understanding how fans appropriate and rework popular culture towards their own ends. I still see the tension in my prose, though, between the general and the particular, a tension Matt Hills (2002) critiqued with pinpoint accuracy in *Fan Cultures*.

How Fandom Studies Emerged from Cultural Studies

I am sometimes called "the father of fandom studies," a title which makes me uncomfortable. From the start, fandom studies as a subfield of cultural studies was profoundly shaped by feminism (and queer theory) and no one wants to be the patriarch of a feminist field. In the same year that I published *Textual Poachers*, there was also significant work on fandom published by Camille Bacon-Smith (1992), Constance Penley (1991), Lisa Lewis (1992), and others, who also helped shape the emergence of fandom studies from older traditions of audience studies. Of course, we were not the first to write sympathetically and knowingly about fans as cultural producers. We were, however, writing about fans and fandom and not constructing a more abstract conception of media spectatorship.

Our books, **Fandom as Audience** and **Fandom as Subculture,** walk us through how the cultural studies frameworks lay the groundwork for the emergence of fandom studies. Much like cultural studies, fandom studies start with a focus on collective behaviors rather than individual ones, seeking to understand what we share with others in our communities and only then trying to understand the choices we make to set ourselves apart and personalize our surroundings. Following Fiske, fandom studies considers the process of meaning making and its relationship with pleasure: how do fans, within a consumer economy, take cultural materials that were mass produced, mass distributed, and mass consumed, and make them our own, use them as resources through which we connect with each other, forge a shared mythology, and construct shared identities.

As we discuss in **Fandom as Audience,** Raymond Williams – the founder of the cultural studies tradition – moved the study of culture away from a select canon of remarkable and accomplished works towards an understanding of culture as "ordinary" and a more anthropological understanding of culture as a shared way of life within a particular people. All cultures, Williams argued, were worthy of study and deserved respect. Stuart Hall (1980) introduced the study of "encoding and decoding" through a focus on media producers and media audiences. He did not see mass media as simply imprinting its meanings on our minds but rather stressed the active and diversified ways audiences construct meanings from the texts offered to them. Hall showed that different audiences made different meanings from the same text so some might embrace dominant meanings, some might resist them, but most negotiated their relationship to their lived experiences. Successful media properties were thus understood not as appealing to the lowest common denominator but rather as appealing to a coalition of different audiences, each finding there something that they found meaningful and pleasurable. This distinction matters because the first leads to cynical efforts to lower popular culture to reach all consumers, while the second encourages producers to deepen and layer their products so that they provide inclusive space for a range of different viewers and their cultural interests.

Hall also promoted the study of representation and fantasy, suggesting that popular culture constitutes a theater where we act out our dreams and where we imagine other possibilities for our lives. One can make a case that fandom is the primary space where these processes are performed in contemporary culture. Fans are drawn towards works of popular culture that give shape to their fantasies, sculpt their desires, encourage the free play of their imagination, and offer us shared resources where we can invite others into our fantasy lives. Magic, for example, offers a powerful metaphor for thinking about power, who has it, and how they choose to use it.

I have argued that fandom emerges from a mix of fascination and frustration: if the objects of our fandom did not fascinate us, we would soon grow bored with them, especially in a world overflowing with diverse media options, marked by cultural plentitude. If they did not frustrate us, though, in some way, we would not continually rework them, a process central to fandom. This frustration might reflect the ways that the potential of a premise is not fully achieved, an aspect of a character is not fully explored, a storyline is not fully developed, or the world is not fully explored. Beyond that, we may find ourselves in tension with the ideologies promoted by a series that we otherwise appreciate or let down by certain songs by a performer whose work otherwise satisfies us. All of this falls under the definition of negotiation that Hall (1980) provided us.

Producers often find fan expressions of frustration and outrage confusing: why are these fans so harsh and critical? Aren't they <u>fans</u>?

Yet this is to assume that fans are all-supportive, that they do not have ambivalent feelings about the culture they consume and that they do not disagree among themselves about what is valuable within a particular work. Fan criticism is often an outgrowth of fan investment; they care enough about a fan object to want to see it achieve its full potential rather than settle for sloppy seconds. They express disappointment because they care enough to set high expectations for the things they love. An early book in fandom studies was called

The Adoring Audience (Lewis, 1992). This title is misleading since adoration is only one pole in the push-pull that makes fandom such a dynamic space.

More and more, audience engagement has become the core currency that drives the entertainment industry. The shows that have the most engaged fans are often those that enjoy the greatest and most enduring commercial success. Engaged fans demonstrate a range of traits that create value within the entertainment industry: they show loyalty to particular television programs, tuning in every week or to particular performers, buying their albums and tickets to their concerts.

Fans actively promote the things they care about to family, friends, and coworkers. They go online and try to publicize what they like about them. They seek out other content through other media channels. And they support brands that attach their messages to the franchises they value. Over the past two decades, we have moved from the era of appointment-based television to the age of engagement-based television, much as we have shifted from broadcast and other legacy media to narrowcast and streaming media content.

In the effort to foster fan engagement, producers are increasingly deploying transmedia practices of storytelling and promotion, dispersing their content across multiple platforms and tapping the affordances of different media. Transmedia depends on a new model of the audience, one which sees consumers as having different degrees of engagement in the story, the world, and the characters.

Transmedia producers and marketers develop strategies that reward these different degrees of investment. These strategies allow some casual viewers an easy and superficial relationship with the content while providing ways for fans to drill deeper and extend their experiences as they pursue "Easter eggs" or explore "rabbit holes," which prolongs their commitment to the content.

Fandom as Subculture discusses what fandom studies took from another important strand of research that emerged from the Birmingham School of Cultural Studies focusing on subcultures. Dick Hebdidge (1979) discussed subcultural style as reflecting conspicuous forms and rituals of consumption. He was interested in how subcultures defined themselves around the objects they consumed, the fashion they wore, the ways they used them, and the meanings and values they expressed through them. He studied how youth subcultures, such as the punks, drew objects from their parent cultures and resignified them, helping them speak to the things that mattered to a different generation.

Subcultural fashions helped to differentiate members of subcultures from those who do not belong, creating a strong sense of affiliation and connection amongst participants. Hebdidge saw the dominant culture as managing resistant and spectacular subcultures in two different ways – provoking moral panics that ostracize members of a subculture as somehow outside the norms of their society or appropriating subcultural symbols as the basis of commodities that might be marketed back to those who helped to bestow them with values.

Fandom studies, thus, starts with an attempt to understand the rituals and practices of fan communities, as they appropriate and resignify various forms of popular culture. The subcultures Hebdidge and his other contemporaries in the Cultural Studies tradition researched were overwhelmingly male, embracing "outlaw" forms of masculinity, which they most often performed in the streets and in public.

Why I Call Myself an Aca-Fan

Angela McRobbie (1991), another British scholar, focused attention on female forms of subculture she suggested were more often performed in the privacy of the home, since women often faced greater pressure to stay off the streets and remain in the domestic sphere. She emphasized the bedroom cultures of teenage girls, whom she called "teeny boppers," what they did at slumber parties, how they decorated their walls, and what records they enjoyed. As such, she was making some vital steps toward the study of fandom and paving the way for the focus on women fans in the first waves of fandom studies.

Moreover, McRobbie called attention to the ways male sociologists, such as Hebdidge, sought to distance themselves from their own associations with the subcultures they studied. Rather, McRobbie embraced a feminist stance where the personal is political and where acknowledging your own positionality, one's relationship to the objects of study, brought new sources of knowledge to their scholarship. She saw this transparency as an ethical set of practices.

Here, McRobbie helped to inspire what has become known as the Aca-Fan stance, the recognition that the scholarship in fandom studies reflects a particular epistemology, ways of knowing which stem from our dual identities as fans and academics. Being an aca-fan means being honest about how we know what we know about fandom. It also holds us accountable to the people we write about and those we write for; both fans and academics seek to better understand how fans relate to popular media.

I have, throughout my career, closely identified with the term "Aca-fan," so much so that I am often described as its originator, but I was not. There had been an early internet group which restricted its participants to those who were credentialed as academics, immersed in fandom, and born female. My early work was controversial as a man writing about mostly female fandom. My wife had taught me different modes of fan interpretation. I had always been comfortable being friends with women. And I applied my empathy and curiosity to do the research. I was certainly a fan but I also was relying on a range of mentors and sources in fandom to help me better understand its practices and logics.

Having worked so hard to gain access and knowledge, and to respect the community, I felt that being denied entry to this online list was unjust. So, I helped to organize a short-lived discussion list, Acafan-L, involving mostly fans working on graduate degrees exchanging what we would today call "meta" comments. I didn't coin the term, but unfortunately, I don't recall who did. I did not use the term in *Textual Poachers*, even though I discussed the concept. The key transition came with my book, *Fans, Bloggers, and Gamers*, where I embraced this identity in print for the first time and then the launch of my blog, which was for fifteen years called *Confession of an Aca-Fan*.

My place in fandom has become much more widely accepted through the years, as has the concept of the Aca-fan. In 2011, I hosted a forum on my blog involving many leading fandom scholars to discuss how they understood the term and whether they found it helpful in defining their own scholarly personas. As some have pointed out, my formatting of the word (Acafan, Aca/Fan, Aca-Fan) has been inconsistent. Ralph Emerson said a foolish consistency is the hobgoblin of small minds. Perhaps this is a foolish inconsistency.

I am settling on Aca-Fan for this book with the hyphen intended to express the distinct but joined subjectivities and epistemologies that fandom and academia represent: the two are coming together, both are part of how I approach the problem, but they do not always sit easily alongside each other. One way we find the space between the two is through autoethnography, as we surface and account for our memories and experiences as fans in relation to the theoretical and methodological insights we have access to as academics.

Understanding, for example, that I grew up as a monster fan may help you understand how I understand fans through a lens of DIY creativity. But it may also be idiosyncratic as data about culture unless it is coupled with larger conceptual and historical frames. In this case, we have several historical accounts of how widespread monster fandom was in 1960s America and the factors – such as the sale of syndication packages to local television stations and how they were programmed into after school strips – which led to it being so (Heffernan, 2004)

Participatory Culture

Textual Poachers introduced the concept of participatory culture that shaped so much of my future work. I claimed that fans were producers (of meaning, of media) as much or more than they were consumers. They wrote and shared original stories – fan fiction – inspired by the media they watched. They created videos that shared how they saw the television they watched. They expressed their identities as fans by making costumes. They wrote and performed distinctive forms of music that were extensions of the worlds they inhabited through their fantasies. They built platforms through which they might share their creations with each other and provide feedback to others who have made things, helping them to acquire more skills and fully reflect the tastes and interests of their communities. They did so by drawing resources from media texts they did not produce and did not own, which was what made them "textual poachers." This focus on fan productivity sets fandom studies apart from the study of audiences or subcultures. Audiences interpret; subcultures appropriate and resignify; participatory cultures create.

Textual Poachers was written at a moment when the era of print-based fandom was about to end and published at another when digital networks and platforms were starting to call greater attention to diverse forms of vernacular creativity, whether on YouTube, where multiple communities of amateur and semi-professional media makers came together and learned from each other's examples, Etsy, which provided a platform for crafters to sell what they made and to trade tips with each other, the dance or lip sync practices that have taken shape around TikTok, or the forms of modding cultures that took shape around games and gaming.

Science Fiction Audiences, the book I co-authored with the British audience researcher John Tulloch, closely followed *Poachers*. I discuss in **Fandom as Audience** the differences in the ways Tulloch and I approached the project and how those differences reflected the methodological assumptions that distinguished fandom studies and audience research.

Fandom is the most researched form of participatory culture and fans use all of these and many other platforms, but not all forms of participatory culture can be described as fan culture. As my understanding of participatory culture grew through consideration of a broader range of examples that the digital age made progressively more visible in our lives, I was asked to write a white paper for the Macarthur Foundation, *Confronting the Challenges of a Participatory Culture*, which linked what we were observing in the field with a growing body of research on new forms of media literacy and participatory learning practices. Here, educational policy was being modeled on ideas that had emerged from fandom studies. Mimi Ito, a colleague in the Macarthur work, and danah boyd, a former student, sat down with me for an extended conversation which formed the basis for our dialogic book, *Participatory Culture in a Networked Society* (Jenkins, Ito and boyd, 2015), a great entry point for understanding the policy and pedagogical implications of our work. This strand of my research surfaces in **Fandom as Participatory Culture.**

Why Star Trek Still Matters

Rob has shared his version of how we met. Here's mine. *Textual Poachers* was still new, and with it, the experience of being a published author, so I was regularly doing an ego-scan on the internet in those days. Robert's site was not up for long when I stumbled upon it and reached out to connect with what I saw as a kindred spirit. One mystery here: "Cyberman" was not my username but my son's, so I am not sure how I ended up writing him on that account.

We started talking online and I was flattered when he asked me to be on his dissertation committee. I did not have any graduate students of my own at that point. I would eventually create a MA program in Comparative Media Studies at MIT and later leave to go to USC when MIT refused to grow it into a PhD program. Rob's was the very first PhD committee I ever served on.

Star Trek was what brought us together and it remains an important reference point across this series. *Star Trek: The Original Series* was among the first television series to develop a distinct, organized fan community. Star Trek fans were major innovators in fan culture, helping to develop practices ranging from fan fiction to letter-writing campaigns to amateur video productions. And the earliest writing in fandom studies largely centered around Star Trek fandom. There are certainly other key touchpoints in the history of media fandom – including *Man From UNCLE*, Star Wars, *Buffy the Vampire Slayer*, Harry Potter, and the Marvel Cinematic Universe, among many others, We try to give them their due, but Star Trek remains a core example because it allows us to trace how fandom and its relations to media producers has shifted over time.

My students often ask me with some panic whether they need to be experts on Star Trek to understand fandom studies. My response is no, because the field diversified with time. However, yes, it certainly might help you understand how debates around Star Trek helped to shape the early development of fandom studies.

From *Convergence Culture* to *Spreadable Media*

As I served on Rob's dissertation committee, I learned so much by reading my work through the lens of consumer studies. Rob's dissertation introduced me to the research of my then-MIT colleague, Eric Von Hippel, who was doing his own parallel exploration of grassroots and open innovation. Soon, Eric and I were walking and talking along the banks of the Charles River. His work surfaces multiple times across the book series, especially in **Fandom as Co-Creation.**

Rob and I lost contact for a few years. I stumbled onto his new work on online communities and netnography as I was sitting down to write *Convergence Culture: Where Old and New Media Collide* (Jenkins, 2008). That book sought to address a core paradox: on the one hand, some were discussing the growing power and concentration of mass media, the idea that a smaller and smaller number of companies were controlling the mediascape and that this allowed for greater coordination across media platforms—what I would call transmedia. This rang true to me.

At the same time, many were saying that the average person had greater access to the capacity to produce and circulate media than ever before, signaling the emergence of what I would call participatory culture. And this also rang true to me. So, *Convergence Culture* discussed the collision of these trends, and in doing so, I was focusing on franchises that had strong fan followings – *Survivor, American Idol, The Matrix*, Star Wars, Harry Potter, and the Obama campaign. I was lucky to have chosen franchises that still hold active fan interest to this day.

After the book's launch, my work received growing interest within the industry—from content companies and strategic communication folks alike. So, I formed the Convergence Culture Consortium and invited Rob and others, whom I considered the most innovative scholars of fans, consumers, and the new media landscape, to join.

Many insights to emerge from that consortium run across this series, updated to reflect the current moment. Most important in those projects were the ideas about grassroots circulation that would form the basis for our book, *Spreadable Media: Creating Meaning and Value in a Networked Culture* (Jenkins, Ford, Green, 2013). This was my first book to be explicitly addressed at least partially towards a corporate readership. Our core theme was deceptively simple: If it doesn't spread, it's dead. We see everyday consumers exerting greater influence on the market and the public sphere through their capacity to spread media throughout their social networks.

When USC was searching for a new endowed chair of strategic communications, I encouraged Rob to apply. I have been delighted to teach a Fan Relations class through the strategic communication program with him twice so far. Our core insights on fan relations took shape in the classroom as we bounced our own thinking, built across two careers, against some truly remarkable and engaged students.

Fandom and the Civic Imagination

Convergence Culture had ended with what turned out to have been a key prediction: that young people were acquiring skills through their experiences as fans and gamers that they would later deploy in more serious realms of education, politics, work, and religion. I was invited to participate in another MacArthur-funded research network that sought to map the connections between participatory culture and the political engagement of American youth. We were finding that young people were seeking to make social change "by any media necessary" and that being able to express their perspectives on current issues within their own networked communities increased the likelihood that they would engage in more institutionalized forms of politics also.

For almost two decades, my former MIT student Sangita Shresthova and I have run the Civic Paths research group at the University of

Southern California. Our evolving understanding of participatory politics, founded on core insights from fandom studies, has inspired three books, *By Any Media Necessary: The New Youth Activism* (Jenkins et al., 2016), *Popular Culture and the Civic Imagination: A Casebook for Creative Social Change* (Jenkins, Peters-Lozario and Shresthova, 2021) and *Practicing Futures: A Civic Imagination Action Handbook* (Peters-Lozario and Shresthova, 2021). Shresthova has also extended our framework through application at the Salzburg Academy, which brings undergraduates from around the world together each summer to sharpen their media literacy skills. She discussed these aspects of our work in *Transformative Media Pedagogies* (Milhailadus, Shresthova, and Fromme, 2022). More recently still, we have been translating these insights into an incubator program for media artists from the Appalachian region as they seek to insert their stories and concerns into the national agenda.

Fandom as an alternative social space allowed participants to get a taste of what a more utopian realm might feel like, with the capacity to imagine a better world as a fundamental step towards working to build one. In my research with Shresthova, we consider fandom as fostering the civic imagination, as serving many of the needs that political scientists have identified as fundamental to social movements.

Some groups, such as the Harry Potter Alliance (now Fandom Forward), have modeled how fans' cultural commitments can lead the community to act in common cause with other activist groups. For example, we consider how *Black Panther* became an important resource in recruiting and educating people about the Black Lives Matter movement.

More and more young people around the world are conducting politics through a vernacular of pop culture references and memes and through the infrastructure provided by fandom. Attend any of the protest movements of recent vintage and you will see people, who may or may not be fans per se, using references to children's books, cartoons, superheroes, or science fiction movies as metaphors for discussing the core issues of our time.

Adventures in Global Fandom

In recent years, my research on fandom has taken yet another unexpected turn. I was invited to spend seven weeks in Shanghai teaching a class on western fandom studies. *Textual Poachers* had finally been translated for the Chinese market. Just before the pandemic, the Chinese state had shut down Archive of Our Own, which I had written about as a site where young people were acquiring a range of different literacies and competencies. See a fuller discussion in **Fandom as Participatory Culture**. The Chinese media sought me out for comment, making me a minor media figure, at least among Chinese fans. However, I did not feel I knew enough about Chinese fandom and wanted to learn what I could on the ground.

When I was not in the classroom or giving talks around the region, I was in the field trying to map the current state of Chinese fandom and popular culture guided by the remarkable Lenore Wang, herself a gamer, cosplayer, and fan of *Doctor Who*, *Good Omens*, and Disneyland, among so much more.

Fandom as Agent of Globalization and **Locations of Fandom** reflect the new thinking that emerged from my close engagement with fan cultures in East Asia. Rather than understanding these viewers as dupes of a global media economy, Fandom Studies encourages us to understand how this content gets localized at the point of consumption, how audiences make their own meaning of content produced elsewhere for other audiences and make these texts their own, much as Stuart Hall had suggested about domestic content decades ago. Our book on Globalization closes with the proposition that the era of American media dominance is ending.

The United States still has a strong role to play in the global media economy, but for the foreseeable future, most likely for the rest of my lifetime, the media landscape is going to be dominated by Asian media producers – Korea, Japan, China, and India now, with Thailand and Vietnam likely to assert more presence in the coming years. There will be shifts amongst these countries in terms of which exerts the greatest market share at any given moment but they all will demand a certain share of interest from fans around the world. And occasionally, countries from other regions – Turkey or Nigeria, say – may break through this Asian dominance..

Their governments will jump on this bandwagon in the spirit of promoting "soft power," a more dispersed version of the old cultural imperialism arguments. This soft power, though, is going to depend on the interplay between immigrants and what I call pop cosmopolitans, i.e. fans who are seeking escape from the parochialism of their own culture through the embrace of pop content from other parts of the world.

My insights here have been shaped by my role in organizing a network of scholars – students and faculty – from both the United States and East Asia who are studying the phenomenon of Transcultural Fandom. Once again, my core partner in this research has been Sangita Shresthova. Her own early work on the transnational dance cultures that have grown up around Bollywood films, Is *It All About the Hips?: Around the World with Bollywood Dance* (Shresthova, 2011), helped lay the groundwork for this work, and she has worked hard to keep India and other South Asian media producers in the mix as we have sought to better understand the flow of media products and fan practices across the Asian Pacific Rim and into the United States.

My childhood and adolescent experiences as a fan, my continued participation in fandom have paved the way for a career focused on participatory culture. My research on fandom has taken me to many different places and I have been able to help expand the space of fandom studies to encompass an ever-broadening range of topics – from fandom as a subculture to fandom as a global phenomenon, from fandom as a site for cultural production to fandom as a driver of education and politics. All of these themes, and many more, will help to inform the Frames of Fandom series, which reflect our priorities as scholars.

CHAPTER 5:
Fans and Fanship

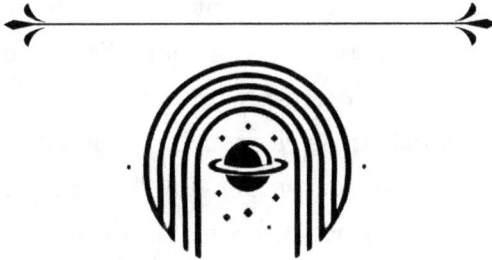

s our autoethnographic introductions demonstrate, we both have long histories as fans. As well, as you can probably tell, there is no shortage of enthusiasm around that topic for either of us. It's safe to say that the subject fascinates both of us. If philosophies express the love of knowledge, then a philosophy of fandom should express not only core principles about what we mean when we talk about fans and fandom but also some of the affection around the knowledge that goes with them.

We are going to spend some time in this chapter providing clear definitions and terms that will demarcate the conceptual terrain of fandom. We will begin at the broadest level of consumer culture, then move into mass culture and popular culture. After that, we will set out, define, and attempt to clearly explain some of the key terms in this book series: fan, fanship, and fandom. We will follow with some thoughts about the continuum that links these core concepts.

Consumer and Mass Cultures

Our autobiographical reminiscences about our youths as fans show that we – all of us – were surrounded by cultural products, some of which we became invested in, engaged with, and fascinated by. These are private inner worlds, personally significant experiences, that we also share as entertainment or entertaining cultures we consume. Whether Henry is talking about *Batman 66*, Soakies, or *Famous Monsters of Filmland* magazine, or Rob is discussing *Gilligan's Island*, Jimi Hendrix, or AMT models, we are also talking about commercial products made meaningful through personal association and everyday practices. Although clearly artistic, creative, and cultural products, films, television, music, and sports are produced by businesses. It may go without saying that they are commercial offerings that are financed with the intention of monetizing them in order to turn a profit.

Consumer culture refers to cultural resources that come from the industrial marketplace, which has been a conspicuous part of Western global society since the 1940s. People are consumers not simply when they buy something or use it up, but when they interact with those cultural resources. One prominent theory of advertising holds that mass media advertising attaches various meanings to products, such as high status for driving a particular kind of car or wearing a particular fashion brand, and people then consume those meanings when they display and otherwise use those products or brands (McCracken, 1986). People use those cultural resources, things such as images, role models, ideas, values, styles, sayings, and objects, and they make them a part of their own lives because consumer culture has both individual and social meanings. People use the cultural resources of consumer culture through various kinds of actions or practices, and they do it because they find them helpful to orient themselves in society, communicate with others, and make sense of their experiences and lives. People have numerous cultural resources to draw upon, besides consumer culture, of course. National culture, family culture, local culture, ethnic culture, religious culture, and other types of culture are certainly rich sources of meaning, identities, and practices that most of us turn to all the time. But so is mass culture.

Mass culture is a subset of consumer culture that refers to the cultural resources created by mass media and often consumed by a significantly large number of people across different societies. The concept emerged with the post-WWII rise of mass production and mass media technologies, such as television, radio, and cinema, which allowed cultural products to be consumed on an unprecedented scale. Some of the key characteristics of mass culture are its commercial nature, the standardization of cultural products, and its wide appeal and accessibility. Often, these characteristics lead to critiques that mass culture is overly homogenized, mindless, and manipulative of public taste.

However, the interesting thing about mass culture is that it does not always stay as mass culture. Like straw magically spun into gold, some of it becomes transmuted. As Henry has explained, building on John Fiske (1989) and Stuart Hall (2006):

> "Mass culture is culture which is mass produced, mass distributed, and mass consumed, but mass culture provides us with the raw materials from which popular culture is formed. On an everyday level, things become popular culture when they become reference points in our conversations. They become popular culture when they become resources when we take them up and use them to make sense of our identity or the world around us." (Kozinets and Jenkins, 2022, p. 267)

As the stories, symbols, language, and other elements of mass culture are taken up by people, they become transmuted into popular culture. The same types of meaning transfer that happen through advertising happen through mass culture as well. When Henry displays his Aurora Wolfman model, or when Rob draws a figure of Howard the Duck into one of his paintings, they are consuming the meanings surrounding these popular culture figures; they become resources that allow them to draw on certain feelings, times, and ideas.

Obviously, certain types of mass culture may tend to appeal more to certain categories of people, who then may turn it into popular culture. The producers of sports, music, and entertainment have particular people in mind when they target, create, and release their cultural productions. There is a long history in Cultural Studies, beginning with the Birmingham School, that studies how certain mass culture products are used by certain races, ages, classes, genders, and subcultures. We will be delving into these topics across the book series and probably go deepest into the topic in **Fandom as Subculture**.

Economically, popular culture is also highly significant. In *The Entertainment Economy*, industry consultant Michael J. Wolf (1999) asserts that, in post-Internet times, the entertainment industry has become "the driving wheel of the new world economy" (p. 4). As we think about how products, services, and brands interrelate with various

ON CONSUMERS AND CONSUMPTION

In fields such as sociology and communication, "consumer" is a term loaded with ideological baggage. Indeed, many scholars actively avoid using the term consumer or consumption because they are wary of its associations with capitalism and the possibility of their knowledge contributions being appropriated for exploitative, profit-making purposes. Henry was one of the co-authors of *Spreadable Media: Creating Meaning and Value in a Network Culture* (2013), a book that consciously avoided the use of the term throughout for precisely these reasons. They felt that the term "consumer" implied that people wore down or used up the objects they consumed, whereas they felt it was important to stress the ways that fans amplified, circulated, increased the value, and expanded the meanings of the works they attached themselves to.

However, our use of the term "consumer" across **Frames of Fandom** draws from the field of consumer research, a sub-field of marketing that freely casts a critical eye on advertising aspects of both the entertainment industry and the economy, it is clear that much of our daily consumption now involves the vibrantly playful elements of popular culture. Popular culture has several other interesting characteristics besides. Because it is pervasive and based on mass culture, it is accessible to a range of people, from different genders, races, orientations, and economic and social classes. Pop culture can both reflect and also influence the everyday lives of people. It can both mirror social and cultural norms and challenge them, providing a platform for social commentary and change. Because it is both ubiquitous and constantly becoming re-attuned to prevailing trends, it may have a strong influence on how individuals and societies understand themselves and each other.

Fan Objects and Fan Culture

No one is a fan of consumer culture or mass culture in general. Fans are fans of specific things on which they fix their interest and fascination. It could also be a particular sport, say baseball or cricket. It could be a specific musician like

and marketing practices and assumes a neutral stance when examining consumer culture that is open to the fact that it has both beneficial and harmful effects on individuals, communities, and the planet. For well over three decades, consumer researchers have examined some of the misleading dichotomies that have led to the stigmatization of consumers and consumption as useful conceptual terms. According to Firat and Venkatesh (1995), a key element has been the foundational premise that production is a value-creating activity, while consumption is value-destructive. The dichotomy between economy and culture, or economies and communities, also mirrors that production/consumption dichotomy. Consumers were assumed to be passive, isolated individuals, not unlike the ostensibly duped and hypnotized television watchers of early media studies. As well, and as we will discuss in greater depth in **Fandom as Consumer Collective,** production historically tended to be associated with the male gender and consumption with the female.

The overall implications of these distinctions were to suggest that consumers do not produce anything of social use or value but are mindless shoppers and passive, isolated users who simply use things of value. However, our more informed understanding of the term consumer refers to the identities and activities relating to how people interact with consumer culture, which is "a social arrangement in which the relations between lived culture and social resources, and between meaningful ways of life and the symbolic and material resources on which they depend, are mediated through markets" (Arnould and Thompson, 2005, p. 869).

To ignore the fact that much of human life now depends on resources that are mediated through markets is to not only deny but also to miss a range of important insights about power, values, and meaning in contemporary society. Decades of research into consumers, brand relationships, and fandom have revealed the immense richness of the world of consumers and consumption. That world is one in which consumers are often active, collective, and creative. Alongside the occasional heedless or impulse purchase, consumers make many sophisticated choices. Consumers are also not always isolated; they often operate as members of families or peer groups. In their various market-mediated acts of consumption, consumers produce conversations, meanings, images, symbols, social media posts, and much more. Consumers, it turns out, are highly productive. And whether we call them "prosumers" (Toffler, 1980) or "produsers" (Bruns, 2013), their various activities and identities are important not only to business and economics but also to our understanding of what it means to be an active member of society today.

Louis Armstrong or a type of music like the blues. It could be a franchise movie series like Avatar or a television show like *The Walking Dead*. It could include theme parks, celebrities, politicians, new anchors, or other popular figures, products, brands, or services. Fans can be fans of people, places, things, and experiences, too, but fandoms are usually intimately linked to popular culture, the reception of the contents of mass culture, and the products of consumer culture. You might be a fan of many different types of media content or branded products.

Let us call the focus of a fan's passionate interest—for example, Harry Potter, the LA Lakers, or *The Beatles*—their "fan object." We could think of the collective usage of the subsets of cultural resources carried by fan objects as "fan culture." Fan cultures contain recognizable elements that also arouse enthusiasm in fans. So, in Star Wars fandom, the fan culture might include personalities such as the honorable Mandalorians and the adorable Grogu, images like Leia's hairstyle or her skimpy *Return of the Jedi* "slave girl" costume, or words like "wookiee" and "droid," elements of this mass cultural offering that have passed into popular culture where their meanings become a type of cultural currency.

In our era of mass digital and consumer culture, the variety of fan objects is wider than ever before. Fan objects permeate entertainment and easily stretch to toys, games, automobiles, motorcycles, recreational vehicles, and so on. We have groups of people who are avid about Minecraft, Monopoly, Barbie, or Lego. Some people are fans of trains who perform trainspotting practices (Tsuji, 2012), or fans of planes doing plane spotting (Lichter-Marck, 2016), or fans of extreme weather events. Then there are fans of material goods—things that one touches, experiences, and tastes, like muscle cars, pinball machines, or French Burgundies. Brands like Apple, Nike, and In'n'Out also have fans. Fan objects are all around us.

In our stories above, you can count many fan objects, from Planet of the Apes and the Chicago Cubs to Patti Smith, Dracula, and Batman. Almost certainly, Gentle Reader, if you are living and breathing in this wonderfully storied world of ours today, you will now be thinking of your own unique list of fan objects. You are, most likely, a fan.

Defining a Fan

A "fan" is someone who is passionately engaged with a fan object. Passion means that the fan object arouses enthusiasm, love, or very strong and even intense emotions. Passion's root word is suffering, and some fans, like a sports fan or perhaps any dedicated fan, may "suffer" because they are fans of that fan object. Fans exhibit relatively strong and usually sustained enthusiasm and admiration for their fan objects. There is also a self-identification aspect. Fans consider themselves to be fans and usually declare themselves to be fans. Being a fan is an identity, not an imposed state.

Music and sports have long spurred fan behaviors. Franz Liszt, the 19th century Austro-Hungarian composer and pianist, had a large female following known as "Lisztomanie." These fans would swoon and throw their clothes at the stage during his performances and, according to historical scholars of fandom such as Daniel Cavicchi (2014) and Hannu Salmi (2020), the term "Lisztomanie," which translated into *Lisztomania* in English, helped establish the blueprint for the modern fan-celebrity relationship. Here, Salmi (2020, p. 55) expounds on the complex set of social, cultural, psychological, and technological circumstances surrounding the "emotional contagion" effects of Liszt's live performances in Europe in the 1930s and 1840s.

> "Liszt was a generator of emotionality whose gravitational field lured members of the audience, drew them closer, but also relieved them again after a while . . . the audience that was thrilled on Liszt's bravura and his skillful tricks on stage, the audience that expressed its emotions through shouts and gestures, and developed distinctive practices of fandom. . . [The] early nineteenth-century culture. . . lived in the process of continuous becoming, structuring, and restructuring due to the cultural explosion with its new forms of communication and transport. In this setting, an emotional aggregate called Franz Liszt reached its affective contagiousness far beyond his physical body, his musical impulses, and the societies where he resided and traveled."

Photography had not yet been invented in Liszt's time, but in the color lithograph of a Lizt performance in Berlin, shown in Figure 5.1 and likely dating from 1847 (Salmi, 2020), we see the same largely female crowds pressed tightly together, screaming their enthusiasm, throwing things on stage, with some of them swooning from emotion that would later be associated with Elvis Presley and Beatles concerts.

Figure 5.1: Franz Liszt performing in Berlin, circa 1847
(image from Lebrecht Music & Arts).

When contemporary forms of capitalism and commercialism encompassed culture industries like music, sports, and entertainment, they increasingly noticed the financial potential of fans. Being a fan is the very essence of brand commitment; commitment is loyalty; and, in marketing terms, loyalty means that you retain existing customers, which requires much less marketing budget than trying to attract new ones. In general, the goal of marketers' "engagement strategies and tactics is to help foster and create a platform where consumers will respond collectively with a deep emotional response" that is reminiscent of the state of being a fan and that exhibits "loyalty, commitment, dedication, [and] devotion" (Kozinets 2014, p. 167).

The qualities of the fan are qualities that contemporary marketers search for and highly value in their customers: customer lifetime value, zero replacement costs, steady, predictable revenue, and calculable goodwill. A lasting and loyal relationship between a consumer-fan and the intellectual property of a fan object has distinct economic consequences for the owner and the consumer-fan of that property. Thus, identifying fans matters to fan object marketers and those whose businesses may depend on them (bar owners near stadiums, merchandise manufacturers, publishers, for example). Identifying as a fan shapes and contributes to the flows of popular culture, consumer behavior, and the mass media landscape. Although the economy is a supposedly rational system, the idea of being a fan throws a blazing spotlight on the passionate and intensely emotional basis of our contemporary "entertainment economy" society.

As sports fan researchers Reyson and Branscombe (2010, p. 177) state, "Any individual who is an enthusiastic, ardent, and loyal admirer of an interest can be reasonably considered a 'fan.' These authors also call fan objects "objects of interest" (p. 190). Indeed, it could well have been the plenitude of fan relationships that Susan Fournier was writing about in her ground-breaking analysis of consumers and their brands when she stated that

> "At the core of all strong brand relationships was a rich affective grounding reminiscent of concepts of love in the interpersonal domain. The affect [emotional energy] supporting brand relationship endurance and depth was much greater than that implied in simple notions of brand preference. Informants in strong brand relationships felt that 'something was missing' when they had not used their brands for a while. Strongly held brands were characterized as irreplaceable and unique to the extent that separation anxiety was anticipated upon withdrawal. Feelings of love ranged from warmth and affection to passion, infatuation, and selfish, obsessive dependency." (Fournier, 1998, p. 364).

Fournier's work told us that people loved brands the way they loved people – for better or for worse, in sickness and in health. Like Rob and Henry did, many people gained their brand relationships from their parents, friends, partners, or other people close to them. People could have many relationships with their brands, including casual friendships, committed partnerships, marriages of convenience, rebounds, flings, enslavement, and secret affairs. Rob and Henry's accounts of their own fan status demonstrate the variety of relationships they have with various fan objects, which leads us to believe that the variety of brand relationships also applies to fan relationships. As noted above, Rob very much wants to illuminate the immense potential in combining what we know about fan culture with what we know about consumer culture.

There is passion in a fan's preference for their fan object. They passionately prefer it over things which are not objects of passionate fan attraction, or even competing fan objects like a rival team, franchise, or musician. That which the fan sees as competing with, opposed or threatening to their fan object may arouse scorn and derision. FC Barcelona fans don't just prefer FC Barcelona, they despise Real Madrid. In Fournier's research, people didn't just prefer some brands, it turns out, they sometimes deeply hated and loved them totally. They had complex relationships with them, different relationship trajectories that sometimes ended in dissolution or forced breakups, and varying levels of self-connection, intimacy, and interdependence. Henry, for example, recalls the warm nostalgia he feels when he sees the Quaker Oats man, feelings that link back to Christmas break in childhood, which were the only times when his mother would serve him warm oatmeal for breakfast. Just as we may pick lint off of our loved one or criticize them for recurring faults, we may love a brand or a media object and be critical of some aspects of what is being done in its name.

Ruminating and expounding on similar topics, in Jenkins (2007, p. 364), Henry asks: "Who isn't a fan? What doesn't constitute fan culture? Where does grassroots culture end and commercial culture begin? Where does niche media start to blend over into the mainstream…?" The meaning of a consumer overlaps heavily with what a fan is: someone who engages with mass and consumer culture and gains a passionate engagement or abiding fascination for their fan object, which is also a consumption object and a mass culture and popular culture production. This drive, this desire, this pleasure instinct, and this keen interest lead them to be fans. Perhaps the most important signifier of whether someone is a fan is whether they declare themselves to be one. We cannot necessarily measure passionate engagement from the outside; it is internal, a felt state; like love itself, it must be declared to reach its full flowering.

Varieties of Fan Engagement

If being a fan means having a passionate engagement with one's fan object, then it is important that we understand what we mean by engagement. Engagement can be highly varied.

A fan's engagement with their chosen "fan object" manifests in multifaceted and profound ways. Considering some of the examples from Rob and Henry's auto-ethnographic recollections, we can see a large variety of ways in which they engage and have engaged with various fan objects.

We can begin by discussing that Rob dreamed about different TV series, such as interacting with Gilligan's Island castaways. Non-physical, imaginary, and psychological, this sort of subconscious and conscious working with fan objects is certainly an important engagement. Imagining scenarios, planning, and daydreaming about the fan object are all forms of engagement that fans may have. These activities point beyond the imaginaries of fandom to its emotional component. With their status as fans defined by their passion for the fan object, fans invariably develop strong historical and emotional connections. Feelings of joy, nostalgia, and even the psycho-therapeutics of personal growth often wrap around fan experience.

Engagement can be intellectual as well as emotional. Fans may dive deep into the grounding, philosophy, thematic, or narrative elements of their fan objects. Sports fans might research the rules and science of their favorite sport. Fans might also engage with the history of their fan object, delving into its background and evolution and appreciating its context and trajectory within the wider power-laden cultural and media landscape. Fans might be curious about media production processes and read behind-the-scenes works (like Rob did with the *Making of Star Trek* books or Henry did with *Famous Monsters of Filmland*). Some fans enjoy analyzing and dissecting every detail of their fan object, from the outcome of games, playlists of concerts, and character development to thematic elements and engineering designs, which is why things like Star Trek blueprints and technical manuals have been popular offerings. Fans can explore different theories and critiques that elevate their understanding and appreciation of their fan object and its various intertextual linkages. This can be a highly intellectual and critical activity that can involve repeated rounds of researching, reading, comparing, watching, and listening.

Then there are the collecting, saving, and curating kinds of activities in which many fans engage, often tied to nostalgia. This kind of engagement involves cataloging and preserving fan-related content, such as clipping and saving pieces of media in a scrapbook, bookmarking key websites, or screenshotting images and texts from social media posts. Fans often collect clothing, books, memorabilia, limited editions, toy figures, signed photography, video or audio recordings, or other items related to their fan object. For some, this may be a very casual or minimal type of engagement. For other fans, it could involve the expensive and careful pursuit of rare or significant items and be deeply personal and solitary.

Collections are curated and they may also be displayed. Fans might also decorate their personal spaces, such as homes or offices, with posters, action figures, and other memorabilia. This kind of display can serve as a daily reaffirmation of their connection to the fan object. For example, Rob recently hung a limited-edition animation cel depicting Bugs Bunny, Daffy Duck, and the Tasmanian Devil dressed as members of the Toronto Blue Jays baseball team in his living room. The cel brings him happiness every time he walks by it because it reminds him not only of his love for the Blue Jays and Warner Brother cartoons, but also of his father, who owned the cel and had it displayed prominently in his home.

Collecting involves buying behaviors, but it can also lead to selling. As Rob did with his father in the past, being a fan can mean becoming involved in marketplace activities as a dealer or seller. Being a dealer involves careful purchase, often some travel, inspection, developing taste, handling the product, caring for, storing, sorting, curating, and displaying the product. Many of the small businesspeople involved in the resale side of the fan culture, people such as sport memorabilia shop, music store, and comic book shop owners, are themselves fans who came to their economic activities via their passionate engagement with fan objects.

Fans often engage with their fan object by wearing merchandise like t-shirts, hats, or other accessories that proclaim their allegiance and affection. The act of wearing symbols of their fan object allows them to visibly carry a piece of their passion into everyday life, often serving as a subtle invitation for recognition from fellow fans. As the examples of bookmarking and screenshotting given above demonstrate, collecting, saving, archiving, and curating behaviors extend into digital formats. Fans can engage by customizing their virtual spaces, such as through social media profiles or desktop wallpapers that depict and reference their fan objects. These forms of display are largely individualistic. However, they serve as powerful means of self-expression and identity formation within the fan's daily life. They may subtly communicate the fan's interests to the outside world, or not. Sometimes they may foster connections with like-minded individuals without the need for active community participation or creative contribution.

There are, as we cover in this section, a vast number of different ways that fans can express their passionate engagement with a fan object. The collection example points to another way that fans can engage with their fan objects, which is by shopping, searching for, and purchasing products and services. Engagement within the vastness of the marketplace can include everything from shopping for a new sports jersey to placing sports bets to subscribing to a pay-per-view event to traveling to see and experience a new sports museum. The market for entertainment and ancillary services is vast and the ways to engage with it are multifaceted and often very fulfilling to fans. Fans may seek immersive encounters such as attending live events or finding virtual reality or other immersive experiences that may allow them to experience the fan object with intense absorption and engagement. Fandom can involve traveling to sites that are important to the content or creation of the fan object. For example, some Harry Potter fans travel to Oxford to tour the university where some of the movies were filmed. Jimi Henrix fans might travel to Renton, Washington, to visit his burial site and the elaborate memorial to him in the Greenwood Memorial Park cemetery.

Mary Louise Pratt (1991) began her oft-cited essay, "Arts of the Contact Zone," by describing the things that her son, Sam, and his best friend, Willie, acquired from their boyhood infatuation with baseball card collecting:

> "Sam and Willie learned a lot about phonics that year by trying to decipher surnames on baseball cards and a lot about cities, states, heights, weights, places of birth, and stages of life. In the years that followed, I watched Sam apply his arithmetic skills to working out batting averages and subtracting retirement years from rookie years; I watched him develop senses of patterning and order by arranging and rearranging his cards for hours on end, and aesthetic judgment by comparing different photos, different series, layouts, and color schemes. American geography and history took shape in his mind through baseball cards. Much of his social life revolved around trading them, and he learned about exchange, fairness, trust, the importance of processes as opposed to results, what it means to get cheated, taken advantage of, even robbed. Baseball cards were the medium of his economic life too. Nowhere to learn the power and arbitrariness of money, the absolute divorce between use value and exchange value, notions of long- and short-term investment, the possibility of personal values that are independent of market values." (Pratt, 1991, 33)

Pratt maps how collecting baseball cards motivated and shaped her son's learning, as his fan object opened him up to larger and larger sets of interests.

The same would be true of adult fans also. Janice Radway (1991) discusses, for example, how reading romances led the adult women included in her study to learn things about geography and history that had not captured their interests when they were exposed to them through formal education. When fans seek out information online in response to their engagement with their favorite television series—Netflix's *Lupin,* say—they find themselves learning more about the original French novels and novelas about the thief but also about French art museums and the landscape of Paris where his heists were staged. A similar grid of associations led Henry from his childhood love of monsters to a broader interest in American film history and, from there, to graduate school in Cinema Studies. And fan fiction writers may push this even further as they resituate the characters in different contexts and do the homework necessary to make these new contexts feel compelling and convincing to their readers.

The example of the fan fiction writer above suggests something further about possible forms of engagement—that engagement motivates and is expressed through various forms of creative expression. Engagement may take the form of something as intangible as backyard play cultures or action figure play as children perform their understandings of the shows they watch on television. Henry wishes he could recover scripts or scenarios capturing what he and his friends did with Batman, the Universal Monsters, or *The Wizard of Oz* when he was little. These forms of creative reworkings can take ever more elaborate forms. Henry (Jenkins 1995), for example, described how online fans of *Twin Peaks* came together to form more sophisticated theories of who killed Laura Palmer, theories that stitch scenes and dialogue together but also speculate well beyond whatever could or ever was shown on screen. When do these elaborate fan theories become a form of fan fiction?

His work on fandom has long stressed forms of grassroots expression and vernacular creativity that are extensions of fan engagement—from fan art to cosplay, from fan music to video production—and it is not hard to see how these interests could be traced back to the wide array of remix practices, amateur performances, and media making he enjoyed in his youth. The British sociologist David Gauntlett (2007) has written much about the creativity of ordinary people, whether in the forms of crafting or personal expression, of home decoration or playing with things like LEGO. One of his essays begins with the question of "how circumstances transpire for everyday hobbyists, tinkerers, and other makers to see themselves as creators." (Culpepper and Gauntlett, 2024). His work also considers the opposite: what happens to leave so many of us feeling we are not terribly creative—to transform children who draw as freely as they breathe into adults who claim to lack any discernible artistic talent. Gauntlett defines everyday creativity as "a process which brings together at least one active human mind and the material or digital world in the activity of making something. The activity has not been done in this way by this person (or these people) before. The process may arouse various emotions, such as excitement or frustration, but most especially, a feeling of joy. When witnessing and appreciating the outcome, people may sense the presence of the maker and recognize those feelings" (Gauntlett, 2018, p. 87). Fan creativity, or what Henry calls participatory culture, is a subset of Gauntlett's everyday creativity. The most elaborate forms of fan creativity—writing and publishing full-length novels—may be associated with the most hardcore fans, but other forms— American children dressing up for Halloween (such as Henry's Keystone Cops) —are more widely dispersed across our culture.

This spectrum of engagement not only enriches the fan's own personal experience but also actively contributes to the evolving narrative and cultural footprint of the fan object itself. In the next section, we take a brief detour from our conceptualizing of the fans to explore one recent example of just such an immersive fan experience.

Sleepover Fans and AirBnB's Icons Series

In 2024, an American tourism and hospitality company, Airbnb, began offering their 'Icons" series in which fans are offered unique, immersive experiences in specific locations. The series offers a range of extraordinary experiences that cater to various interests, including sports, media, and music. These experiences are not only about staying in unique fan object-related locations but also include interactive and personal encounters with famous personalities and settings. The experiences cater to the interests and passions of fans, offering them a connection with the narratives and characters they have known and loved for so long. By doing so, Airbnb not only acknowledges the importance of the fan in contemporary culture but also enriches it by providing fans with a new way to engage with their favorite stories.

For instance, fans can sleep in a unique bedroom at the Ferrari Museum in Maranello, Italy, which is filled with race cars. Fans of Prince can stay in an exact replica of the house featured in Purple Rain, located in the music icon's hometown of Minneapolis. Wendy Melvoin and Lisa Coleman of *The Revolution* hosted the experience, which included listening to unreleased music from Prince's vault. The TikTok influencer Khaby Lame, a popular content creator, offers an experience that celebrates his love for manga. Guests are invited to stay in a specially designed gaming loft in his hometown of Milan, Italy where they can dive into his personal fandoms. Comic book fans can book stays in locations inspired by the *X-Men '97* series, and animation fans can stay in the *Up* house from Pixar (which is lifted into the air using a crane) or control room from *InsideOut 2*. Each stay is meticulously crafted to provide a unique and interactive adventure where fans can experience life as the characters they admire and even encounter fictional characters like the X-Men's Jubilee or Pixar's Carl Fredericksen.

It is worth noting that these experiences are not auctioned to the highest bidder, as they might be on eBay. Instead, and remarkably, most of these experiences are priced under $100 per guest, with some even offered for free. However, there's a catch—and an interesting one! Fans interested in these stays must go through a competitive process where they express their enthusiasm and reasons for wanting to participate. This involves filling out a detailed statement of interest when requesting bookings, almost as if they were applying for admission to an exclusive club or university. Only a few are successful, and this competitive aspect seems to be an attempt to ensure the presence of fans who will most deeply cherish these experiences (and perhaps talk about them the loudest and most eloquently!). It seems that these experiences are designed to be more than just commercial transactions; they are meant to be profound, special cultural experiences, differentiating them significantly from typical commercial theme park offerings which are open to even casual or disinterested consumers.

Experiences like sleeping in Prince's bed or experiencing your *Up* house being lifted far into the air were once the stuff of dreams and imagination. Today, they are carefully crafted into tangible commercial realities that leverage the passionate engagement of the fan. In AirBnB's case, the entertainment connections are also superb branding—they elevate the brand to the realm of fantasy in ways that would otherwise be impossible. As we consider these unique offerings— from intimate concerts in living rooms to nights in recreated worlds of beloved characters—we can recognize them as vivid illustrations of novel types of engagement for fans to experience.

Being a fan is no longer about admiration from afar. Fans today seek and want to get up close with their fan objects. In this case, settings from these fan objects become objects that you can stay and sleep in. Travel consumer fans are offered immersive engagements that honor and celebrate the cultural phenomena they cherish. Increasingly, media producers recognize how special these experiences can be. Where once they were mass-produced and cheaply merchandised, now they are constructed as special and unique. They are limited editions. You need to apply or win a golden ticket. Or, perhaps, like an overnight stay in the whimsical "Up" house, they are designed to be priceless.

Fanship

The ways a fan can engage with their fan objects may easily transition into the realm of the social. Rob and Henry related different behaviors that involved being fans alongside other people who were close to them. Rob discusses watching Blue Jays baseball games and episodes of *All in the Family* with his whole family gathered around the television set, telling fibs to friends at school about being related to Carolyn Jones, and going on weekly pilgrimages with his friend to see the Jimi Hendrix and Led Zeppelin double feature. Henry writes about acting out *Batman* in his backyard with other kids in the neighborhood. He and his brother would jump

IMMERSIVE FAN EXPERIENCES

In using the term "immersive experiences" here and elsewhere across the book, we do not mean to simply refer to "immersive theater," a genre of popular performances that removes the separation between audience and performers, brings theater into distinctive real-world environments, and allows for unscripted interactions. Janet Murray uses the term more expansively in her groundbreaking book on digital aesthetics, *Hamlet on the Holodeck*, suggesting that "we seek the same feeling from a psychologically immersive experience that we do from a plunge in the ocean or swimming pool: the sensation of being surrounded by a completely other reality, as different as water is from air, that takes over all of our attention, our whole perceptual apparatus" (Murray, 1997, p. 98-99).

We are using the term here to refer to the profound, intense, and participatory pleasures of being a fan. In that sense, immersion may stem from properties of the performance context, as in immersive theater, properties of a medium such as VR or AR that seem to engulf us inside a fictional world, properties of audience engagement, or even properties of branding as discussed in relation to Campfire Media's multi-layered model of media consumption in **Fandom as Audience**. In *The Art of Immersion*, Frank Rose (2012), for example, describes the expansive, accumulative narratives associated with transmedia entertainment and the participatory cultures that surround them as immersive, even though the immersion may only be into the realm of the fan's imagination. This relates directly to our conception of imaginative processes such as dreaming and daydreaming as noteworthy types of fan engagement.

on the bed to the rousing *Batman* theme song. As if gathering in a type of local juvenile mini-convention, he would meet with kids in his tree house, read comics, and discuss new superhero adventures.

Sports researchers have long used the term "fanship" to refer to an individual's sense of connection to a sports team (Gantz and Wenner, 1995). Reysen and Branscombe (2010) broadened the use of the term to include anyone who is devoted to an interest, which could include entertainment, music, or celebrity interest. They used social psychology theories to explore the nature of fanship, viewing the ideas as related to how much a person feels psychologically connected to a sports team. Reysen and Branscombe developed and validated a psychological scale to measure fanship among sports and other types of fans, a category that included fans of television shows, music groups, and hobbies. Their research found that fanship was characterized by emotional connection, investment in the interest (in terms of money, time, and energy), identification with the interest, and affiliation with other fans. Those who scored higher on fanship had held the interest longer, spent more time participating in their interest, expressed more willingness to participate in fan activities, and had more friends who participated in their fan interest.

Intriguingly, a person's fanship was also correlated with their sense of "entitativity"—which is the degree to which they view a fan group "as a distinct entity" (p. 185)—and also the extent to which they identify with the fan group. As the authors put it, "greater fanship was related to more fan behavior, and a greater desire to keep non-fans at a distance from one's life" (p. 184). As well, fans perceive themselves to be in a fan group "even when they are not actively participating in one" (p. 187). The concept of fanship also includes "co-viewing" experiences (Gantz, Fingerhut, and Nadorff, 2012, p. 65). For sports fans, these co-viewing experiences include watching sports with other people at home, in sports bars, at stadiums, and "electronically" on cell phones and social media sites. The concept of sports fanship also extends to posting, commenting, replying, and generally having discussions online with other fans (Lewis and Gantz, 2019).

So, although being a fan and engaging in fanship are considered largely individual pursuits, fanship has a definite social dimension. Human beings are social animals, and popular culture is, by definition, something that is shared. Therefore, it seems sensible to recognize that there is a certain social dimension to many forms of fanship, which can include co-viewing, co-listening, or otherwise co-enjoying the fan object with other people. There are fans who enjoy discussing their fan objects with friends, family, and coworkers. Fans may get together en masse for sporting events like the World Cup games, for music performances, and to see entertainers. Fans might also involve their friends in a neighborhood game of Planet of the Apes, Batman or take them on other fantasy-fuelled adventures.

Equally compelling is Reysen and Branscombe's (2010) finding that fanship is interrelated with both the person's tendency to view a fan group "as a distinct entity" (p. 185), a real thing and also the extent to which they identify with the fan group. Sandvoss (2005) has suggested that fans understand themselves to be associated with fan groups even when they are not actually connected to any fan organization. These understandings may be related to the idea of an "imagined collective," which is defined as "a collection of individuals who do not interact synchronously with each other, and who presuppose the existence of the collection of individuals who share the same common ground" (Kashima, Klein, and Clark, 2007, p. 35). Fans partaking in fanship also partake in the imagined sense that they belong to a larger collective of fans who share an interest in and enthusiasm for the fan object.

Rhiannon Bury (2018) argues convincingly that the fandom studies literature has been characterized by a false dichotomy of participatory and non-participatory fans, which had the effect of narrowing the emerging field of study. To remedy the situation, Bury proposes the following:

> "I suggest that participation be understood as a continuum: the practices that require the least amount of involvement in participatory culture on the one end, such as information seeking, and those requiring the greatest amount of involvement on the other, for example, producing fan works as part of a gift economy (Booth 2010). Following Jenkins, I do not consider regular committed viewing of the primary text to be participation in itself but rather recognize it as the baseline practice that distinguishes fans from 'bystanders.'".

We agree with Bury's proposal for a "participatory continuum" and will visualize one later in this chapter. It makes good sense to carefully examine the variety of fan practices in context. By doing so, we might see how certain practices may be related or might often lead to other ones. The types of behaviors and thought processes associated with being in a state of fanship contain intimations of being involved in wider fan collectives. Henry's gathering of friends in his treehouse to read Batman comics might anticipate collective activities of fan clubs and conventions. Fans might be aware of wider collectives and identify with them in some ways, but that does not indicate that they are affiliated with those collectives. However, despite the grassroots creation of hierarchies, such as the Geek Hierarchy, that try to place different types of fans in a status-based relationship with one another (Busse, 2013), we suggest resisting the temptation to conclude that one type of fan practice is better or closer to an ideal than another.

Because we are discussing ideas involving individuals, social collectives, and their interrelationships, there are persistent paradoxes pervading our understanding. Running through these notions are the tensions that mark the division between a community and a mere grouping or identity category. We draw inspiration here from Arthur Koestler's (1978) social notion of "the Janus Principle." The Janus Principle dictates that every fundamental element of a structural system in a social hierarchy has the Janus-faced principle of looking out for its own autonomy and also seeking to join with other subsystems. The individual in society is always caught within this integrative tendency to function as a part of a larger whole, balanced with a self-assertive tendency that seeks to preserve the freedom of individual autonomy. This is the tension between being a fan, engaging in fanship, and having a sense of participation in fandom; it is the omnipresent tension between acting as an independent individual and as an organized member of a collective. We will see this principle play out in many ways through this text, which was the product both of a holistic partnership between two (generally) like-minded thinkers, and also of two careers of individualized and specialized scholarly thinking.

A final, particularly gray area is the role of online participation. Lewis and Gantz (2019) consider posting, sharing, commenting, replying, and generally having discussions on social media with other fans to be examples of fanship. Bury (2018, p. 129) differentiates between more and less participatory online fans, suggesting that those who lurk might be different from occasional posters and those who engage in "regular, sustained interactivity" online. Her analysis seems to suggest that we not treat all types of online participation as equally participatory or non-participatory. It seems obvious to us that someone who runs an online K-pop fan site keeps a mailing list, organizes fans, and informs them about upcoming concerts and events is engaged in far more collective work than someone who occasionally goes to a social media site to read discussions about their K-pop band's latest song release. Both may be important activities contributing to life as a fan. However, the latter activity seems much more related to fanship, while the former is suggestive of fandom.

CHAPTER 6:

Fandom

Defining Fandom

In his autobiographic recollections above, Rob relates how, at around the age of 12, he began regularly attending science fiction, comic book, and Star Trek conventions. These spaces were social. Seeing the many people who shared a variety of fan object interests, he realized something that he had only read about before, namely, that there were groups of people out there who shared their fascinations about these things with each other. It introduced him to fan discussions, fan fiction, fan art, and numerous other activities that he had been pursuing in a solitary fashion and with select friends. Later in his recollections, he relates how he and his friends would regularly attend baseball games and music concerts and events. Being at these live events again brought him into contact with others who were enthusiastic about the Blue Jays, Chicago Cubs, and various music bands. Although it wasn't until his dissertation work that he joined a local Star Trek fan club, Rob had numerous points of contact where his status as a fan of specific fan objects brought him together with other fans.

Henry writes that he was attending the Atlanta Fantasy Fair by the time he was an undergraduate, and, a few years later, was reading fanzines of various kinds and actively engaging with a fan community. He discussed the role of fan fiction in his relationship with his wife, Cynthia. He talks about engaging in cosplay, and his regular attendance at fan conventions, from the large to the small.

Rob and Henry's auto-ethnographic recollections recount them joining in with collectives of other fans, learning about and participating in the culture of these collectives. The conceptual sections above define being a fan and fanship as forms of passionate engagement with a fan object that exists as a production of mass or consumer culture. However, the culture that fans create for each other extends beyond and, in some ways, exists apart from the mass or consumer culture products that bring them together. Engagement with other fans of the fan object and with their culture—its dynamic system of values, language, identities, roles, rituals, stories, images, histories, personalities, and other shared symbols and their meanings—is at the core of fandom. For the most part, what sets this book series apart from dominant industry models for audiences is that we are less interested in individual decision-making and viewing than we are in the larger social and cultural context that fandom provides. Keeping this collective social and cultural context in mind, we will next provide a few illustrations to help drive home the core concepts of this book.

The Three-Way Relationship of Fandom

PERSON
("Fan")

PASSIONATE ENGAGEMENT

FAN OBJECT
e.g., Harry Potter, Taylor Swift, Boston Celtics

Figure 6.1: Being a Fan and Fanship

Figure 6.1 is a visual summary of the discussion in the prior chapter about the state of being a fan and being in a state of fanship. It depicts the relationship between an individual and a fan object such as Fifty Shades of Gray, Misty Copeland, or the Chelsea soccer club. The individual has a personal relationship involving their passionate engagement with the fan object. As the prior chapter described, there are many ways that this passionate engagement can manifest, which might include, but not be limited to, engaging imaginatively with the object and watching, reading, listening, collecting, and display-ing things related to the fan object. The core idea in Figure 6.2 is that being a fan and being in a state of fanship are individual matters between a person and a fan object.

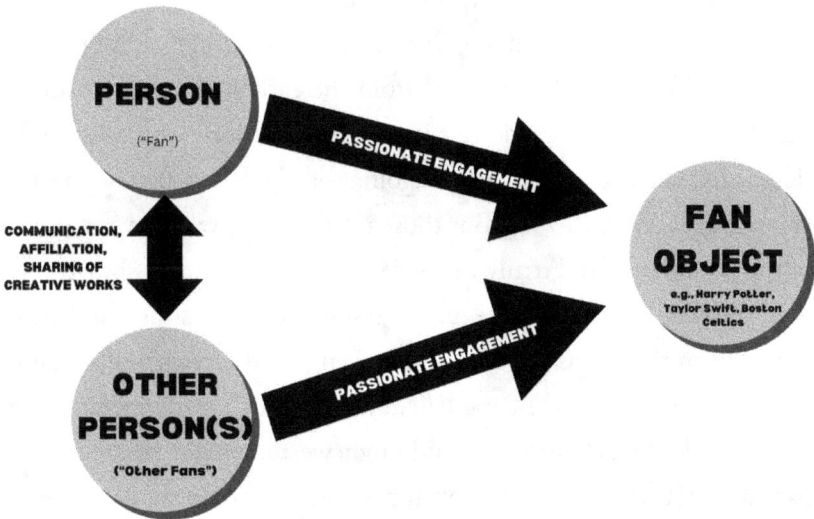

Figure 6.2: Being a Member of a Fandom

Membership in a fandom is depicted in Figure 6.2. The person, or the fan, stands in the same relationship of passionate engagement with the fan object, as depicted in Figure 6.1. Rather obviously, the member of the fandom is also a fan and exists in a state of fanship. However, there are other people, or other fans, who are now involved in the relationship as well. Those other fans also have relationships of passionate engagement with the fan object, although, of course, different fans would not have exactly the same type of passionate engagement with the fan object as one another. The most distinctive element of the figure, however, is the presence of a new arrow, which marks a new relationship. This is the two-way arrow on the left-hand side that connects the fans together. Being a member of a fandom means that the fan is not flying solo anymore; they are part of a group that communicates, affiliates, critiques, shares creative works, organizes, activates, and/or engages in numerous other group activities. That group might include fans, but it might also, especially within a networked culture, include others such as performers or showrunners who regularly attend conventions or post on discussion lists.

Increasingly, people have been referring to these relationships as "parasocial," a term that emerged from the early history of broadcasting to describe the ways viewers imagined television hosts or even fictional characters as engaging in ongoing social relationships with them (Horton and Wohl, 1956). But those relationships were, by the nature of the media involved, truly one-sided. However, when a showrunner goes on social media and regularly responds to questions and comments from their fans (or when people engage there with other fans), those relationships may be mediated, but they are not parasocial. They are actual social relationships, although we may want to specify the particular terms of those relationships more fully than that.

Contrasting Psychological and Cultural Perspectives on Fandom

The sports psychologists Reysen and Branscombe (2010) emphasize the psychological elements of fandom as a form of identification with the group. They assert that "fanship is identification with the object itself, while fandom is identification with others who share a connection with the object" (p. 177). They link fandom with Tajfel's

(1978) social identity theory, where fandom is part of an individual's self-concept that derives from their knowledge that they belong to that group as well as the value and emotional significance that they attach to that membership. Reysen and Branscombe's psychology tests were able to distinguish between fanship and fandom as separate constructs by measuring the extent of individuals' identification with fan collectives.

For Reysen and Branscombe, fans could "reap the benefits of fandom," such as "collective happiness," without "making actual interpersonal connections" (p. 188). Although group identity is certainly one facet of membership in fandom, we view fandom as a cultural phenomenon that contributes a rich mix of activities and experiences that stretch far beyond simply identifying with a group, such as critiquing, organizing, and communicating activities named above. In a digital age, the idea of "making interpersonal connections" becomes somewhat flexible and could include virtual contact without ever meeting face-to-face. For some elements of fandom, it may indeed be possible to reap the benefits through forms of virtual contact; for others, face-to-face contact might be necessary.

In our perspective, which focuses on the cultural, fandom refers to the collective, the group of fans who share a common interest in, enthusiasm for, and engagement with a particular cultural phenomenon, such as a movie, TV show, book series, sports team, board game, theme park, or celebrity. When a fan expresses their passionate engagement with other passionately engaged fans of the object of their fandom, they are a member of a fandom. When they participate in larger fan communities, attend fan events, participate in online discussions between fans, or create fan works like artwork, fiction, videos, or memes, they are members of a fandom. Because it is a collective activity, and that collective can gather online or in the physical world, fandoms have members. People are *engaged* in fanships, but they are *members* of fandoms. It is not only the individual identities that interest us. It is also the broader collectives themselves, what they do, how they function, and what their implications are as collectives and social entities.

We have discussed how mass culture may become transformed into popular culture. Fandom adds a new cultural element. Fandom continues the transmutation process, adding levels of communal involvement and commitment with new contexts, activities, and ways to create and express passionate engagement. The collective and participatory aspects are what makes fandom valuable, both for the participants and for brands and producers who may benefit from such attitudes and activities. But it also may be what makes fans annoying and frustrating to some of those same groups. Fans make demands—if nothing else, they want to be heard; often, they want their tastes and interests to be factored into production decisions.

The Fanship-Fandom Continuum

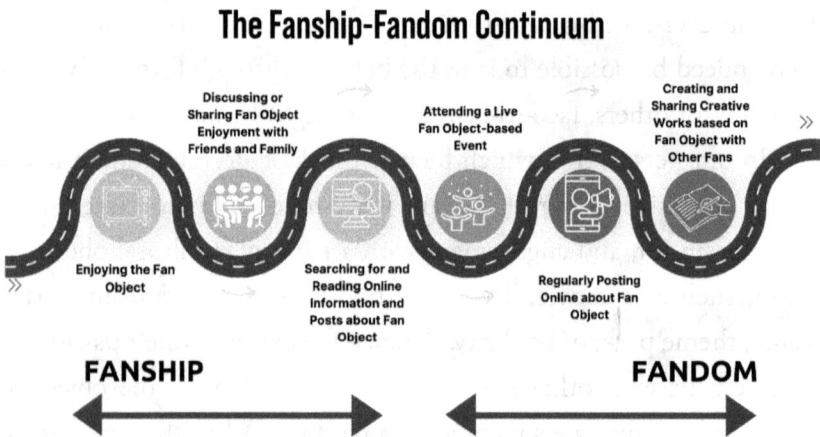

Figure 6.3: A Fanship-Fandom Continuum

Figure 6.3, visualizes fandom's progression as a wavy continuum. The circles represent behaviors that someone might engage in and could lead them to be considered in a state of fanship or membership of a fandom. The six circles are not intended to be comprehensive. They are simply a sampling of a few kinds of behaviors related to fanship and fandom. Many other activities, such as organizing, criticizing, interpreting, and translating, could be included in this diagram. The first circle, the one on the far left, enjoying the fan object, could be considered to be the starting point for becoming a fan. There are many fans who are mainly solitary in their enjoyment and engagement with the fan objects that matter to them and who might never progress beyond that first circle.

There are plenty of fans who enjoy, discuss, or share their fan objects with friends, family, and coworkers but who do not partic- ipate in larger fan communities, go to fan conventions, participate in online discussions, or create fan works. Discussing or sharing fan object enjoyment is depicted as the second circle in the diagram. Although it has a social component, that component does not involve affiliating with or connecting with a collective of fans. So we consider it, like the first circle, to be an activity of someone who is engaged in fanship that largely centers on their relationship with the fan object. In Rob and Henry's auto-ethnographic recollections, there were numerous instances of them sharing their fanship for tele- vision shows or music with people in their immediate social network.

The next circle is where the boundaries between fanship and fandom become fuzzier. The third circle conveys activities where the person begins to search for and read online information and posts about the fan object. Online information and posts certainly could contain a wealth of communication about fan collectives and their cultures. However, because the fan, in this case, is searching and reading but not engaging, this seems to be less about affiliation and connection with the fan collective and more about searching for information about the fan object. Perhaps the posts will contain information about the fan collective, which will interest, inform, and intrigue the fan. Perhaps it will plant seeds that eventually grow into a desire to learn more or to reach out and contact members of the fan collective. However, we believe searching and reading are activities associated more with fanship than fandom.

With the fourth circle attending a live fan-object-based event, our continuum crosses over into the borderlands of fandom. By attending an event such as a concert, a sporting event, or a convention, the fan is put into contact with other fans who are not in their immediate social network. They are exposed to some kind of collective where the members of the collective are united—they are physically co-present, even if only consocially—in their passionate engagement with the fan object. The fan might have limited contact with these other fans, however. Perhaps they only sit next to each other or occupy the same room. The event might be only a very temporary gathering that is over in an hour or two. Still, at this point, the fan is out in the world, co-present with other fans at an event based around the fan object. At sporting events, they are exposed to the uniform wearing, eating and drinking, calls and responses, booing, heckling, cheering, and other behaviors that constitute the local culture at the event. At music events, they will see how others are dressed, the signs they carry, the way others sing along, and other responses to the performers and performances. At live events, the fan will be exposed, even temporarily, to the fan collective and its culture. Because of this, we would classify them, even if only for a short while, as having entered the world of fandom, even though they may not identify with it or consider themselves members. As with the fourth circle, this activity is on the border of the continuum and might be considered a fuzzier classification.

With the next circle, there is commitment by the fan towards a fan collective. When a fan's passionate engagement extends to the collective level of other fans, they become a member of a fandom. That may involve things like rewatching, rewriting, reimagining, restorying, or recirculating. It could be communally buying and selling. It could be organizing events for other fans. The fifth circle relates to a fan who regularly posts about the fan object online. By posting regularly, the fan is expressing commitment. They are passionately engaged with the object of their fandom and they are also engaging with the online fan collective by regularly contributing content to it. This regular contribution constitutes participation in the collective. Even though the participation is online, digital participation is the face of much of fandom today. We certainly would not want to exclude the many committed fans who are organized into online fandoms and so we see this behavior as clearly indicating that of someone who is a member of a fandom.

The final circle, which is firmly established as a behavior that marks membership of a fandom, relates to a fan who creates and shares creative works that are based on the fan object with other fans. In this case, the fan is clearly involved in and participating as a member of a fan collective, a fandom. They are creating something, whether fiction, art, music, informational videos, detailed reviews, translated subtitles of foreign productions, or anything else that might relate to the fan object and potentially be useful to the actual or potential members of the fandom. They could be contributing online or at in-person gatherings; for our continuum model, it does not matter. But by contributing to their creation, they are clearly participating in the participatory culture of fandom.

Varieties of Involvement in Fandoms

As our diagram shows, fandom is a somewhat liquid phenomenon with somewhat unclear boundaries. Fandoms, the collectives, may continue to exist, but the people within them may come and go. Fandoms come and go, too, for many people throughout their lives. What we love most intensely and care deepest about may be limited at any one time. We may have limited cognitive time and emotional energy to invest in these activities at any one time.

There are temporary fanships, local fandoms, and intermittent fandoms. People come and go freely from both fanships and fandoms. You might be in a fandom for a season, and then never again. People might get together in local venues to cheer for their favorite Olympian gymnasts only once every four years. A fan might attend a concert for one of their favorite musicians only when they come to their city. They might hold watch parties once a season or attend a convention only every year. That said, Henry and his wife, Cynthia, have regularly returned to Escapade, a Southern California fan gathering, and seen some of the same people off and on for over thirty years, constituting some of their closest friendships even if they only encounter these people at the con. If we wanted to define them as either partaking in fanship or being a member of fandom, we would need to carefully assess the extent of their participation in the fan collective, in both online and in-person manifestations.

Like maintaining any membership, remaining a member of a fandom requires investments of time and energy. It requires regular engagement, in some ways, with both the fan object and the fan object collective. Whatever the fandom, members of fandom express their fannish enthusiasm through a range of different activities that include collecting, creating, discussing, and participating in events related to their interest in the objects of their fandom. However, as we will see with our exploration of fandom in a range of different contexts, the essence of fandom lies in the emotional connection fans develop with their interests and with one another, fostering a sense of identity, community, and usually some form of creative or critical engagement.

Fandom researchers as well as fandom marketers might consider the utility of charting life cycles by mapping the cultural products that a person consumes with gusto and commitment. Larry Grossberg

(1992) coined the term "mattering map" to refer to the set of things that matter to people and their relation to each other. It may be useful to plot the changing heatmaps of a given fan's desires, their passions, the things they follow, and their fandoms as they burn high and low.

The line between fanship and fandom is not clearly marked, which means that making this determination is a matter of interpretation. When investigating a fandom or its members, you need to investigate its context. It is not merely a matter of a fan attending an event or not, or going to an online fan group or not. There is no magical border or tripwire that one crosses to enter fandom and not all fans will join fandoms. In fact, the vast majority will not.

Importantly, being a member of a fandom is not a destination to which all fans must aim. Being a member of a fandom is inherently no better or worse than being a fan who is enjoying their fanship but is not a member of a fandom. And, although both of us have many years of experience in both fanships and as members of fandoms, we do not believe that there is a hierarchy with members of fandoms on top. Someone for whom the enjoyment of the fan object itself is sufficient is absolutely fine with us.

Five Key Characteristics of Members of Fandom

As we see it, the members of fandoms are the most passionate, connected, creative, critical, and/or active consumers or audience members of popular culture. Fandoms give them an outlet through which they can celebrate, support, critique, reimagine, and derive pleasure from the activities related to their fan objects. Let's explore these five core elements in greater depth.

#1. Members of fandoms are passionate.

Unlike the stale traditional economic models, which assume consumers are isolated, rational individual decision-makers who calculate the utility of products and services, fandom draws our attention to the fiery power of emotions, longings, commitments, and relationships. The enthusiasm of fans for their fan objects brings them together. Once they join as a collective, their enthusiasm is multiplied. Not only does fandom act as an accelerant for individual fan passions, but it also provides new foci for other passions. With the culture, events, information, history, personalities, and activities it offers, fandom itself becomes a key focus for fan attention and a breeding ground not only for fannish enthusiasm but also for fan innovation.

The word enthusiasm comes from the Greek root *entheos*, referring to possession by a god. The concept started out as a religious one and referenced a potent form of spiritual ecstasy and almost overwhelming sense of inspiration. During the religious civil war in England in the mid-1600s, the term became highly politicized and combatants would refer to the Catholics as overly enthusiastic and irrational (Cavicchi, 2014). A strong fandom is something brands want because they have mechanisms allowing them to monetize passion. In *The Culting of Brands: Turn Your Customers into True Believers*, Douglas Atkins (2004) suggests that these enthusiastic passions unite fandom, religious cults, and cultural brands such as Apple and Harley-Davidson. Wildly passionate consumers, Atkins says, have the same rabid enthusiasm as members of a fandom.

Similarly enthusiastic stereotypes later became closely associated with the members of stigmatized and publicly shamed fandoms like Star Trek (Jenkins, 1992). Having strong internal passion in the group means having a strong sense of the outgroup. And, whether these are called muggles, mundanes, or normies, the culture of fandoms helps their members erect defensive boundaries against those who would stigmatize them. Passion, love, and relationships certainly undergird the construction of a fandom and of the strongest brand loyalties. Recognizing that the members of fandoms are invested emotionally, cognitively, culturally, and psychologically—and not just finan-cially—should lead brand managers, consumer culture theorists, innovation managers and theorists, sociologists, and anthropologists to deepen their understanding of this crucial element. If casual view-ers often seem indifferent, the members of fandoms have the "feels" for their fan objects and they express them openly and proudly. We return to and significantly deepen our discussion of the passion of fandoms in **Fandom as Desire**.

#2. Members of fandoms are connected.

All consumption takes place in a social (as well as personal) con-text. Nothing, not the words in our mouths or the clothing on our bodies, is of purely individual origin or is outside of the social sector. Being connected has become a natural part of our everyday lives. Fandom transpires in the digital and physical spaces where fans con-sistently and committedly gather, share, and engage with content, brands, showrunners, media, and, most importantly, one another. These connections are multiplicitous, including traditional physical spaces like conventions, meetups, and retail locations, many of which are more prominent sites of fandom than ever before.

Furthermore, connective digital platforms are the vital backbones of fandom today, serving as the essential infrastructure that supports the creation, distribution, and consumption of fan-related media and activities across global networks. The digital economy facilitates a sub-cultural connection that has proven to be a good growth medium for fandoms and the communication capabilities fans need to construct a sense of confederation. "Networked computers empower people around the world as never before to disregard the limitations of geogra-phy and time, find one another, and gather together in groups based on a wide range of cultural and subcultural interests and social affiliations" (Kozinets, 1999, p. 253). Digitalization, it turns out, is fandomization.

Digital platforms for fandom range from social media sites to specialized platforms like Patreon, OnlyFans and BiliBili. Digital platforms of fandom also include fan sites, streaming services, and even virtual and augmented reality environments. Using these connective platforms, fans seek out others who share their passions and interests. They often discuss, design, develop, and then deploy affiliation and association intensification rituals and practices.

Fandom as Technoculture provides a detailed history and theoretical orientation for these platformized fandom relationships and what we can learn from them. Fandoms become sites of contestation where technologies programmed to monetize fans' individual passions (and rarely their collective ones) must contend with self-organizing collectives that may still, for the most part, be based on moral economy principles. For this reason, fandom's connections and technoculture also lead it to become a staging ground for activist interventions. See **Fandom as Activism.**

#3 Members of fandoms are creative.

Human beings thrive on being active and creative participants in their lives, rather than passive consumers of commercial culture. In contemporary times, commercial culture often provides the raw ingredients–but rarely the recipes– from which to form profound and personally significant meanings. Fandom is a space where these recipes can be shared. Rules can be bent, identities explored, and new possibilities imagined. Playfulness in fan culture, through art, play, hobbies, writing, performing, costuming, filming, photographing, and website and platform design and maintenance allow for experimentation and expression in ways that can challenge, critique, or affirm current realities, both individual and collective. Fans use their fandom to express their interpretations and feelings publicly through making things – objects, videos, fan fiction, fan music, costumes, and the like. We return to this topic in our **Fandom as Participatory Culture** and substantially deepen it there.

#4. Members of fandoms are critical.

Because they care and because they are doubly invested in both their fan object and their fandom, members of fandoms are also the ones who ask hard questions. They form opinions together, a key trait traditionally associated with publics. They are often drawn to a particular fan object because of the conversations it enables them to have and they want to weigh in on the choices being made by brands and producers in relation to it. They are simultaneously the most loyal supporters and the harshest critics of the things they love. We will discuss those aspects in **Fandom as Public**, among other places.

#5 Members of fandoms are active.

Cognitive research on narrative comprehension (Bordwell,1989; Branigan,1992) suggests that understanding even the simplest media text involves complex processes of perception, hypothesis formation and testing, and interpretation. Media consumption is never really passive. But, as we saw above, engagement with a media text inspires a broad range of activities and the deeper you get into fandom, the more complex, prolonged, and perhaps meaningful those activities become. Fans might be personally and passionately engaged with their fan object in ways that could include watching, listening, dreaming, fantasizing, and so on. Many fans might be relatively relaxed about how they express their fanship. Members of fandoms tend to get active with their fanship; they do things with it. If their favorite program seems like it is endangered, they organize campaigns to try to save it. If a new book is released in a favorite series, they may go to the bookstore when it is first released. If a team makes a questionable trade, they might organize a boycott. They circulate information, and if the fan object is in a foreign language, they may participate in a subtitled language translation or "fan subbing" initiative. Their activities may have consequences, whether as supporters of Save Our Show campaigns, participants in boycotts, participants seeking to open markets to global media properties, or educators about aspects of popular culture that may be less known, but which might appeal to a committed fan base. Throughout these books, we are interested in what people do as fans and why they do it.

Passion, connection, creativity, discernment, and activity—these are five core attributes of members of fandoms. These five a ttributes are not static or mutually exclusive; rather, they interact and reinforce each other in complex ways, creating a dynamic and evolving fan experience. For example, a fan's passion for a particular media franchise might fuel their desire to connect with other fans, leading them to participate in online forums or attend conventions. This c onnection, in turn, can spark creativity as fans collaborate on fan fiction, artwork, or other forms of expression. Throughout their various passionate and creative engagements, fans may develop a more critical understanding and discernment of the source material, leading to more informed and nuanced discussions within the fandom. This active participation in the fan community may further reinforce the fan's sense of passion and connection, perpetuating the cycle of engagement.

By examining the mechanics of these five attributes, we can gain a more comprehensive understanding of fandom as a multifaceted phenomenon that extends well beyond passive audiencing or consumption and encompasses a wide range of social, cultural, and creative practices.

CHAPTER 7:

Fandoms in Action: Sports and Music

A Very Short History of Fandom

People have probably been fans since prehistory, drawing elaborate cave paintings of the hunts that engaged their passionate enthusiasm and intense interest. As soon as two cavemen began wrestling and gathered around them a grunting, cheering crowd, we probably had something like fanship. There is a strong historical record showing that there were fans of Roman gladiators who followed the contests and gathered together to cheer on their favorite competitors. Pointing to the pervasiveness of these behaviors, the historian of fandom Daniel Cavicchi (2014, p. 67) writes about the "wide range" of things we might recognize as fan objects, although the specifics of these stories are now lost to posterity.

> An 1873 *Galaxy Magazine* article, for instance, outlined a wide range of cultural enthusiasms going back to ancient Greece, many of which are lost to us now, including "a rosy glow" about mathematics, alchemy, the Holy Land, South Seas speculation, and tulips—or Jenny Lind, Dickens, croquet, baseball, oratory, steamboat

racing, silkworms, and hens in the United States We may
see some of these as short-lived social "fads" rather than
more significant forms of fanlike enthusiasm, but recognizing that distinction has itself helped shape the
broader concept of "fandom."

Not only were there fanlike enthusiasms going back to the time
of ancient Greece, but they included things like tulips, silkworms,
alchemy, and the Holy Land.

According to Cavicchi (2014, p. 67), the historical record surrounding "sports, literature, and theater, together with music, form
the most promising realms through which to historicize fandom."
The fandom of kranks" in American baseball is an excellent example. In antebellum America, kranks were valued every bit as much
as the players on the field. Kranks saw baseball as a social event in
which they had a significant participatory role (known as "rowdy-
ism"). Their "rooting" was as competitive as the players' batting and
fielding. Although krank culture was competitive, it was similar to
the early music fandom because both shared rituals of exhibition and
gender politics. By 1920, kranks were moved away from the field and
into stands, where they could be prevented from interfering with the
game's main spectacle, similar to how music fans were disciplined
into remaining silent around 1900.

This chapter and the following one consider some of the major
fandoms in the world and attempt to sketch out some of their key
characteristics as a starting point for additional discussion. Building
out from the lengthy sections in Rob's recollection about his sports
fanships, particularly his lifelong fanships as a dedicated Blue Jays
(and Chicago Cubs) fan, we will start with what is undoubtedly the
most popular form of fandom in the world and one that will be
familiar to most, if not all, of this book's readers: sports fandom.

Sports Fandom

Worldwide, sport is a massive industry that brings about 6 billion people together–76% of the world's population (though, notably, not Henry)—with great passion (YouGov, 2022). We could argue that sport, or sports (as it is called in America), is a competitive activity that has some type of quantifiable goal or external reward as its focus, which requires physical exertion, and that has the body as its central expres-sive object (Loy and Coakley, 2007). Despite this definition, however, the definition of sports is constantly changing. In Britain, darts are a sport. In America, poker tournaments are covered on national sports networks. In other contexts, chess, and other games, are treated as sport. The 2024 Paris Olympics featured break, or break dancing, as an event. And then there is the burgeoning realm of esports, which some would argue are "real sports," and others would say are videog-ames with a confusing label (Parry and Giesbrecht, 2023).

Carrington and Andrews (2013, p. 3) write that sports are a "space for human creativity and bonding, a physical and competitive art form that shows what the human body –and therefore humanity as a whole–is capable of." Writing with passion, Zirin (2010, np) explains the central role of fans' investments in sports.

> "Sports is as human an act as music, dance, or organising resistance. While sports may, in a vacuum, have no "sig-nificance," the passion we invest in it transforms it. Sport morphs into something well beyond escape or a vessel for backward ideas and becomes a meaningful part in the fabric of our lives. Just as sports such as football reflect our society, they also reflect struggle."

Combining the local, regional, national, and global sports fandom is a powerful and multifaceted experience involving intense

identification, powerful emotions, the adoption of rituals and traditions, and a strong sense of community belonging. Amenta and Miric
(2013, p. 313) argue that it is the "deep connection" to "competition,
with its focus on winning and losing and uncertain outcomes," that
distinguishes sports fans from other fans such as fans of film stars,
rock banks, and television shows." Today, it may also involve wager-
ing in various online and offline contexts, with some of them, such as
sports fantasy leagues, being unmistakably communal and collective
in nature. In fact, Halveson and Halveson (2008) consider sports
fantasy leagues to be a unique combination of learning, play, and
engagement, which they term "competitive fandom."

Sports fans follow their teams with great loyalty. Sometimes,
family ties are strained by the fanship and fandom of one member,
but families are also brought together, with spouses and parents
passing on these affiliations to other family members (Tinson,
Sinclair, and Kolyperas, 2017). For the French sociologist Pierre
Bourdieu (1984), becoming a fan of team sports is a function of
social class, with members of the working class highly represented
as fans, while middle and upper classes tended to play individual
sports into adulthood. Crawford (2003) asserts that sports fans followed a type of "moral career" through the stages of different fan
statuses. Crawford mapped the involvement of sports fans through
fanship and into fandom as follows: from "general public" to "interested," "engaged," "enthusiastic," and "devoted"—categories that
included the vast majority of sports fans–to "professional" fans and
from there to fans who worked in the sports industry. Markovits
and Hellerman (2001) hypothesize about why many people became
lifelong sports fans. They argue that, once one became a fan of one
sport and a specific team within that sport, it was difficult to shift
allegiances or to turn back because of sunk emotional and knowledge investment costs.

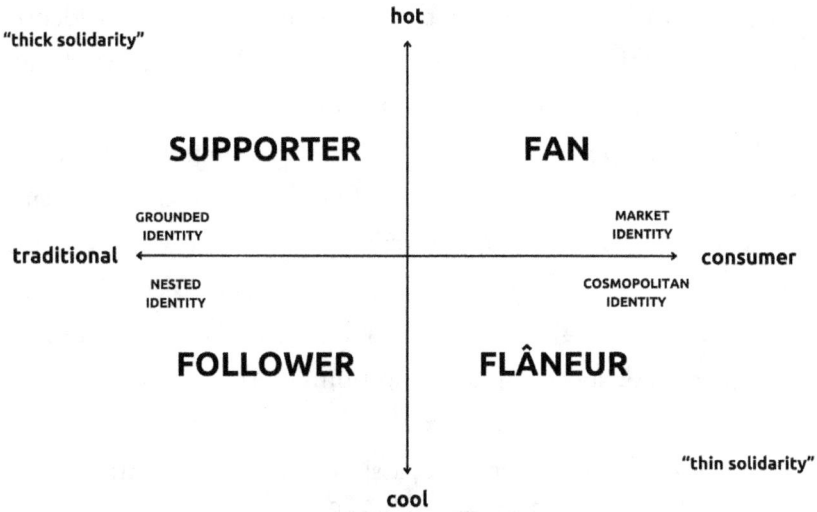

Figure 8.1: Guilianotti's Sports Spectator Taxonomy

Figure 8.1 presents an abbreviated form of Richard Giulianotti's (2002) interesting "ideal type" typology of sports spectators, which he developed to capture what he sees as the commodification and globalization of sport. The typology uses two dimensions of attachment—hot vs. cool and traditional vs. consumer—to categorize sports spectators into four types: supporters, followers, fans, and flâneurs. Supporters resemble our members of fandom; they are deeply loyal, often local, and emotionally invested. They attend games in person and embody a traditional and passionate attachment to their clubs. Followers are more like those in a state of fanship. Although still rooted in tradition, they engage with sports in a more detached, cool relationship, often mediated by media consumption. Fans in this categorization become almost stereotypical. They are characterized by intense, consumer-driven loyalty. They maintain a strong connection to sports but do it through market-based interactions. Flâneurs, who are the most detached of the four categories, engage with sports in a superficial, transient manner, reflecting the increasing influence of globalized, consumer culture on spectator behavior. Giulianotti's categories attempt to uncover the underlying dynamics of identity formation within the contemporary sports world as they are shaped by broader economic and cultural shifts.

Moreover, sports fandom is not merely about the pursuit of momentary pleasures and the thrill of victory. Instead, it is situated in a series of thrills and disappointments, highs and lows, that mirror the rises and falls of significant life experiences. Dietz-Uhler and Lanter (2008, p. 104) overview research that uncovers the emotional consequences of sports fan identification. Sports fans are those who identify with or "establish a psychological connection with the team." They are not mere observers, but passionately engaged participants in the unfolding action. The interactions of sports fans with the network of other fans—in other words, being a member of a fandom—have been linked to fan identification with a team.

> "The effects of sports fan identification on affective responses suggest that sports play a powerful role in the emotional reactions of sports fans, especially those who identify most strongly. For those with a deep psychological attachment to a team, emotions such as enjoyment, happiness, satisfaction, and anxiety can fluctuate dramatically depending on the success or failure of the highly valued team" (p. 107).

The term "tribalism" often comes up in literature about sports fandom. Competitive, local, and emotional, numerous types of identities and affiliations—including ethnic, racial, and class—are often on full display among sports fans and their fandoms. The way the members of sports fandoms dress alike, travel together, chant in unison, react together, decorate their bodies and faces, and affiliate around their team colors and symbols may evoke the impression that they are a tribe. John Hughson (1999) explores the tribal aspects of fandom within Australian soccer's A-League using French sociologist Michel Maffesoli's adaptation of the term in his concept of "neo-tribes". Maffesoli (1996) argues that modern societies are characterized by a shift away from traditional, fixed communities towards more fluid, temporary, and interest-based groupings, which he terms "neo-tribes." These neo-tribes are not based on kinship or geograph-ical proximity but on shared passions, lifestyles, or consumption patterns. In the field of consumer research, Bernard and Véronique Cova, Al Muñiz, and Tom O'Guinn relied heavily on Maffesoli's concepts in their formulations of "tribal marketing" (Cova and Cova 2002) and "brand communities" (Muñiz and O'Guinn 2001). We discuss these concepts in greater depth in **Fandom as Consumer Collectives**.

Hughson examines two distinct types of fandom groups: those connected to long-established clubs with ethnic ties, such as the Bad Blue Boys, who support Sydney United (with Croatian Toot), and newer groups, like the Boys from the Shed, who support teams with-out such ethnic and historical affiliations. The former group's identity is deeply rooted in ethnicity. Bad Blue Boys tend to wear team colors, often combining them with the Croatian flag in a paramilitary-style that reflects their ethnic heritage. They participate in choreographed chanting and display banners that signify their Croatian cultural and team allegiances. The Boys from the Shed, who support Perth Glory, are predominantly of British background. They are known for their vocal and physical presence, creating a rowdy atmosphere in the sta-dium by singing English football chants, waving flags, and adopting a "laddish" style that includes the public display of British identity. Hughson's study emphasizes the dynamic and fluid nature of these neo-tribal affiliations in the context of Australian soccer fandom, revealing how these collectives negotiate their identities and spaces within the broader societal framework, a process that often involves them pushing against rules imposed by soccer authorities in their quest for self-expression. These high levels of adrenaline associated with sports fandom have, in the past, led to unfortunate events such as riots, violence, and hooliganism.

Sports fandom brings people together; it also divides. Mahfound Amara (2008) explains how the "Muslim world has, on the one hand, accepted modern sport as a symbol of modernization in Muslim societies and as a privileged tool for nation-state building. But on the other hand, many Muslims—particularly representatives of Islamist movements—are wary of modern sport as a symbol of secularism and a deviation from the authentic societal concerns of the *Umma* (the nation of Muslim believers)" (p. 67).

"The mass celebration which followed the Iraq national team's victory in the Asian Cup, and the more recent success of Egypt in the African Cup of Nations, are illustrations of the significance of sport (especially soccer) and the symbolic force that it has in mobilizing nations to overcome class, gender, and sectarian divides—at least for the duration of the match. Sport—due to its generalization—also provides for cross-cultural encounters with other people of different cultures and faiths. In this sense, sport becomes a shared form of communication." (pp. 72-3)

At times, sports and sports fandom can serve as sites of racism and misogyny. Because sports have been seen as a masculine domain where ideologies of male superiority and dominance have been structurally and symbolically situated, women have long been excluded from participation in sports, with their interests marginalized and their presence in sports fandom mocked (Esmonde, Cook, and Andrews, 2015). Although there are definite signs that this is changing, women's interest in sports is still frequently ridiculed as allegedly centered on their attraction to male athletes, rather than their appreciation for other aspects of the game. In their Critical Race Theory analysis of Black, Asian, and minority ethnic supporters' experiences of football fandom, Lawrence and Davis (2019) conclude that "football fandom and spectatorship remain predominantly 'White' activities." The result is that Black, Asian, and minority ethnic fans must negotiate and resist a sense of belonging in football fandom cultures. Sports have also become ground zero for tensions and discussion about transgender competitors (Flores et al., 2020).

In an important critique of the "whiteness" of fandom studies, Rebecca Wanzo (2015) cites the example of Gerald Early as an academic whose work on boxing and its followers might otherwise have been valued for its contribution to fandom studies: "Early fulfills the criteria of a fan: encyclopedic knowledge, participation in a community, and productivity as a sportswriter." But he also shows how Black intellectuals often must embrace a more ambivalent perspective than their white counterparts. She quotes Early, "for the black intellectual, boxing becomes both a dreaded spectacle and a spectacle of dread. The black fighter is truly heroic for the black masses and the black intellectual only when he is fighting a white fighter, or someone who has been defined as representing white interests. The battle then becomes the classic struggle between the black and the white over the nature of reality." When fighting another Black man, he becomes someone selfish, preying on his own people. "Moreover, the Black fighter's heroic moment is never one in which he is in control, but simply his own desperate effort not to be swallowed in a sea of black anonymity" (1988, 114).

Sports fandoms are also important sites of contestation and resistance. Using the example of the multiple engagements that Islamic Iranian women have with soccer in their country, Fozooni (2008) illustrates how a gendered fandom interacts with religious identity, national culture, and sports culture to create a site for agency and resistance. "Iranian women's participation in football as rioters, fans, players, referees, coaches, sports writers and administrators of the game," she writes, catalyzes "both Iranian feminism and the wider working-class social movement confronting the mullah-bourgeoisie" (p. 114).

"Tribalism" in the Modern Context: A Critical Reflection

The terms "tribe", "tribal", and "tribalism" have a complex and often contested history. Originating in anthropological studies of so-called "traditional" societies, they have since been applied to various contemporary phenomena, including political affiliations, fan communities, and even the loyalties of brand aficionados. However, this application has not been without controversy.

Numerous Indigenous peoples and scholars have criticized the use of "tribalism" in Western contexts, arguing that it perpetuates harmful stereotypes and trivializes the complex social structures and cultural richness of Indigenous communities. Jodi Byrd (2014, p. 59) eloquently voices some of these criticisms, noting that "US colonial culture continually underwrites its mastery by subsuming and assuming Indigenous markers to define itself." Its use of the term tribal to refer to digital gatherings may therefore serve "to maintain the illusion that new and improved American tribal interests have superseded if not entirely replaced Indigenous peoples," a process they call "Tribal 2.0."

History, unfortunately, gives us numerous examples in which the "tribal"

Music Fandoms

Just as there are many different ways to engage with sports fandom and many different types of sports fans, there are also many types of music fans and ways to engage with music fandom. Yet there seem to be elements of music fandom that have remained constant over what we know of its history. The fandom historian Daniel Cavicchi states:

"I couldn't believe, when researching, say, opera fans in the 1850s, how much they seemed like Springsteen fans in the 1990s. Both were engaged with music in ways that purposefully enhanced its role in their daily lives. I've come to see fandom as a means of approaching the consumption of the arts that involves obstinately remaining in a performance frame when it is no longer there. The struggle to stay emotionally and experientially connected with performers and performances, aside from conventions of exchange set up by service industries, is always there" (Baym, Cavicchi, and Coates, 2018, p. 142).

One can be a music fan by appreciating a particular type or genre of music, such as country, a particular band, such as Blackpink, or an artist, like Bob Marley. Today, however, pop music fandom moves beyond merely appreciating and listening to music. It is often characterized by lifelong, intense levels of dedication and participation, the same as the passionate commitments found in sports fandoms. In their book *Aging, Media, and Culture*, (2014), Denise Bilby and C. Lee Harrington explore the processes by which long-time fans incorporate and adapt their fandom into their life narratives. Music, with its rich emotional resonance and its links to times and social scenes, is

designation of Indigenous peoples was intended to denote primitivism and backwardness, to dismiss claims of sovereignty, and to justify their colonization and marginalization. Furthermore, cavalier application of the "tribal" term to contemporary phenomena runs the risk of obscuring the power dynamics and historical context that shape social identities today. It may also reduce complex group affiliations to simplistic notions of innate group loyalty, overlooking the role of social, economic, and political factors. Finally, as Byrd (2015) notes, the use of the term in a novel way may be viewed as presuming the disappearance or dispossession of Indigenous tribes.

Despite these critiques, we are on the side of those who argue for the term's continued relevance in understanding contemporary social dynamics. We believe that the "tribal" and "tribalism" terms can and should be separated from their colonial baggage and used to describe a specific form of collective identity characterized by strong in-group loyalty, shared values, and a sense of belonging. Psychologists Clark, Liu, Winegard, and Ditto (2019) have gone so far as to declare that tribalism is "human nature." This is a view that must be considered with caution, as it could be used to naturalize racism and segregation and promote a colonialist or universalist view of human nature. Instead, we would counter that these views of "tribal" characteristics do not refer to so-called "traditional" or Indigenous societies but rather to the tendency of some people to form groups based on shared interests, beliefs, or experiences. This tendency manifests in various forms, from sports fandom and political affiliation to online communities and brand loyalties. The connection to our current work on fandom should be obvious.

Although Maffesoli's (1996) use of the term "tribe" has also been subject to critique, his concept highlights the potential for a novel and updated reinterpretation of "tribalism" that moves away from its problematic associations with traditional societies and focuses instead on the dynamics of collective identity formation in the modern world. Maffesoli's reinterpretation aligns very well with our own use of the term "tribal" to describe fandom's loose-knit collective form. This form operates in contemporary Western society, based not on rigid social structures but on shared interests and emotional connections. Thus, please read our occasional use of the terms "tribes" and "tribal" as denoting something akin to the "neo-tribe" and the "neo-tribal" concepts used by Maffesoli and successfully applied to the contemporary consumer culture context.

We acknowledge here that the use of the terms "tribe," "tribal," and "tribalism" in modern contexts remains a matter of ongoing debate. However, what is clear is the need for critical engagement with the term's long history and important implications. Whether using "tribalism" or "neo-tribalism," it seems crucial to acknowledge the terms' contested nature, avoid generalizations, and consider the specific context and power dynamics at

a powerful resource that people use to shape their own identities, alter their moods, and develop empathy throughout their lives. Researchers have found that people's music preferences are established around their late adolescence and early adulthood and generally stay with them for life (Davies et al. 2022). The musical tastes of people over their lifetimes seems to reflect their tastes around their sexual coming of age, which Holbrook and Schindler (1989), who first studied the phenomenon, compared to "ethological studies of imprinting" as well as a peak level of "social pressures from one's peer group." As Bilby and Harrington note, we know much less about what roles music – and other – fandoms play for seniors, though downloading music ranks highly amongst the activities seniors perform online.

The King and the Fab Four

Crowned the undisputed "King of Rock 'n' Roll," Elvis Presley, arguably set the stage for global music-based celebrity culture as we know it today. From his humble Tupelo, Mississippi, origins, Elvis rose to the heights of celebrity in the mid-1950s, mesmerizing audiences with his unique blend of rock, country, and rhythm and blues, a blend that owed as much to Black music culture as it did to his own steamy sexuality and charisma. Elvis's electrifying stage presence, characterized by his gyrating hips and rebellious image, made him a global sensation, particularly among young fans. Young men wanted to be like him, and young women wanted to be near him. Like many musicians before and after him, he role-modeled and embodied sexuality, coolness, attractiveness, authenticity, and much more. His influence rapidly spread from recording and live events across multiple media platforms. Television appearances, notably on "The Ed Sullivan Show," showcased his charisma and fueled his popularity. After conquering television, Elvis also made a significant impact in film, starring in 31 movies that, while often critically panned, were box office hits and served as vehicles to promote his music. Then, from 1969 until his death in 1977, he performed 636 shows at the International Hotel in Las Vegas.

Elvis and his management team pioneered entirely new levels of celebrity merchandising, with his image and name appearing on a vast

play. Doing this will require a nuanced understanding of the different forms of collective identity and the factors that shape them. It should also involve, as it does here, recognizing the disrespect and potential harm that uncritical use of "tribalism" can cause, particularly to Indigenous and so-called "traditional" societies, communities, and their people. Further, this conscious use of the term should consider the Indigenous critique of universalism. It should distinguish clearly between the claim that "tribalism" is innate to human nature and the notion we assert, which is that "tribalism" might be a generative theoretical framework for comprehending the behavior and activities of certain groups of people, such as fandoms.

Thus, by engaging critically and intelligently with the terms "tribe," "tribal," and "tribalism," we can move towards a more nuanced understanding of collective identity and sociality in the contemporary world, one that respects the diversity and complexity of all social experiences.

We thank Sebastian Wurzrainer for insightful comments that helped us shape this sidebar and acknowledge that the views expressed here are those of the authors.

range of products, from clothing to more unusual items like lipstick and shoes. This commercialization created a lucrative industry that set a precedent for future stars. Even after his death, Elvis's brand continues to thrive. Graceland, Elvis's 17,552-square-foot home in Memphis, Tennessee, is a fan pilgrimage site that typically receives more than 600,000 visitors annually. This makes it the second-most visited home in the United States after the White House. His music, image, and memorabilia remain in high demand. In an interview with an Elvis Presley fan, Mark Duffett (2000, p. 85) asked about fans' collective dedication to the superstar. With great passion, the fan replied:

> "It's love for the man. I have got a very deep love for that man. I—I've always said this—I would give my life up now if I could bring him back. I'm not saying that because it can't happen. I'm saying that genuinely because I'm a nobody—that man made millions of people happy, and if I could bring him back, I would sacrifice myself. That's straight up, that is. I've said that for years."

While writing about passionately devoted fandoms, we could also write about the Fab Four–John, Paul, George, and Ringo–and the sensation they caused when they came to America on February 7, 1964. Like Elvis, their lasting legacy also stretched from music recording to film, collectibles, and memorabilia. Their live performances still live on in history as places where the screams of female fans in the throes of Beatlemania were impossible to ignore (they also made it impossible for the musicians to hear themselves on stage). Considering what she calls the "screamscape" of Beatlemania in a feminist and historical context, Rohr (2017) concludes that it was a form of emancipation that presaged and perhaps initiated other freedoms.

"The screaming of fandom was a site of release, joy, and rebellion, especially when individual fandom was enacted in public—at concerts, on street corners, outside hotel rooms, and waiting at airports—and Beatlemania became a broad cultural current. Individually and collectively, these screams made up an important part of the soundscape of the 1960s, giving voice to young people, music fans, and women, and representing an early iteration of cultural rebellion and challenges to the confines of gender in a decade that would come to be defined by both."

It is somewhat mind-blowing, but the Beatles have been associated with a powerful cultural revolution in which their fandom altered the social fabric. As Corry (2010, p. 1) writes, "As both agents and models of change, the Beatles played a key role in establishing three main attributes of the embryonic counterculture: the maturing sensibility of rock music, greater personal freedom as expressed by physical appearance, and experimentation with drugs. United by the goal of redefining social norms, activists, protestors, hippies, and proponents of the growing counterculture found in the Beatles an ideal representation of the sentiments of the times. Embodying the very principle of change itself, the Beatles became a major symbol of cultural transformation and the veritable leaders of the 1960s youth movement."

Deadheads

The Grateful Dead is a powerful example of a music band that built and courted a devoted and long-lasting fandom using unconventional means. Self-proclaimed Deadhead and professor Nancy Reist (1997, p. 183) explains the fandom as follows:

"Many Dead Heads feel they have a kindred relationship with other fans, a bond which frequently is described as a significant part of the Dead Heads' [sic] attraction to the concerts. Communication between fans is rich in mythic symbolism and ritual. Dead Heads share a rhetorical community based in symbolism which is overtly mystical and introduces a mythic dimension to their mundane experiences. For many Dead Heads, the performance itself is only one part of the phenomenon. The interactions between the fans are equally important. Indeed, hundreds of Dead Heads show up for concerts but never actually go inside. Instead, they congregate in the parking lot, forming a Grateful Dead community that follows the band on the road, rather like a traveling band of gypsies.

Business author David Meerman Scott and tech company CEO Brian Halligan (2010) –both self-proclaimed Deadheads as well– teamed up to write *Marketing Lessons from the Grateful Dead: What Every Business Can Learn from the Moist Iconic Band in History*—a key lesson related to ownership and intellectual property rights. While most bands strictly forbid recordings of their live shows, the Grateful Dead were a notable exception. Professional recording artists signed to big labels tend to forbid concert attendees from recording the shows. In fact, there is a history of vigorous, and even violent, enforcement of those no recording policies at concerts. However, in a move that seemingly prefigured the creation of the Creative Commons, the Grateful Dead encouraged their fans to record and share their live music.

Encouraged by the band's permissive policies, fans became custodians of an extensive archive of recorded live performances, meticulously cataloging and then sharing them. Sharing the music required contact between fans, and those contacts created conditions for enhanced fan community. As a result, the Grateful Dead fandom became a vibrant micro-economy that actively traded live show recordings, setlists, and other grassroot-created memorabilia among themselves. This grassroots effort led to developing a network of "Deadheads" who acted as librarians, preserving and curating the band's history. Not only this, but it prompted a lasting culture of connoisseurship and tastemaking, in which fans would recommend certain shows, or even years. Examples of recent online comments include the following:

> "If you like jazzy Dead, 1974 is your year."
>
> "My all-time favorite set has to be 1975-08-13 San Francisco, CA @ Great American Music Hall."

What were all those Deadheads doing in the parking lots of those shows? Among other things, they were listening to, showing off, trading, discussing, and critiquing the many recordings of shows, as well as bartering, buying, and selling a variety of fan-made (and other) merchandise. The Grateful Dead and its management allowed fandom to have its own markets without having to license the action and take a cut. The resultant wealth of fan-driven activities not only deepens fans' connections to the band but also fosters a unique culture of communal exchange and collective memory that sustains the band's legacy to the present day.

From Bob Marley to K-pop

Bob Marley and The Wailers provide a powerful example of a musician who gained global cultural influence through the intercession of an active fandom. Marley's success gave Jamaican music a global profile in an industry that had been dominated by musicians (like Elvis and the Beatles) who originated in first-world countries. His lyrics articulated the concerns of people who were poor and black, colonized people who lived in slums. A result of Marley's success was to inspire the expansion of Rastafarianism within Jamaica (King and Jensen, 1996, p. 18). Furthermore, Marley's reggae brought global attention to Rastafarianism, and his music continues to operate today as an expressive channel for marginalized people everywhere (see O'Gormon, 1997). In her musical fandom ethnography, Baulch (2004) studied Marley and reggae fandoms in the Indonesian province of Bali. Baulch (2004, p. 19) finds that its rise "can be traced not only to the global tourism industry in which Bob Marley's image and music came to be associated with tropical, beachside destinations, but also to more interpersonal encounters between Indonesians, Jamaicans, and other Rastafarian communities abroad." Anthropologists theorize about how individual members of a culture bear that culture and carry it abroad. Apparently, the same processes happen with fandoms.

The powerful influence of music and musicians continues to this day. In their ethnographic work with One Direction, Magcon, and Justin Bieber music fandoms composed of groups of 13- to 14-year-old European girls, Lacasa et al. (2017) found that a panoply of fan discourses contributed to the formation of these girls' individual and collective identities. They included interpreting and sharing fan-made content, such as creating fan art of Bieber and One Direction, writing detailed fan fiction involving them, and producing heartfelt tribute videos, which they circulated online. On platforms like Twitter and WhatsApp, they formed close-knit groups, where they discussed the latest news, organized fan meetups, and carefully retweeted posts from their idols. They would attend concerts dressed in band merchandise, where they would chant lyrics and wave posters, transforming these events into rituals that solidified their fan status. For many of them, the music was linked to significant moments in their lives, offering comfort during tough times. For instance, one teenage fan would repeatedly play a song that helped her through a breakup, creating a strong connection to both the artist and fellow fans who shared similar experiences.

The astounding global rise of K-pop fandom is a testament to the transnational nature and appeal of music and musicians in the contemporary world—and there have been numerous explanations for it. Providing an infrastructural mode, Oh and Park (2013, pp. 389-90), for example, assert that:

> "The rise of K-Pop in the global music industry involves a new technique of locating new musical content in Europe or elsewhere, modifying it into Korean content, and then redistributing it on a global scale. Furthermore, K-Pop represents an effort to network global talent pools and social capital in the formerly disconnected music industry rather than an effort to emulate and slightly modify Japanese pop culture. As such, within the global music industry, Korea occupies a structural hole that exists between Western and East Asian music industries."

On the other hand, Messerlin and Shin (2017) attribute the rise of K-pop to economic advantage by Korea in entertainment production and distribution, including the cost effectiveness of streaming technologies. On yet another hand, Choi and Maliangkay (2014) praise the South Korean government for creating synergies between K-pop and other media and culture industries such as radio, television, film, advertising, and live concerts. Interestingly, as discussed above, these interrelations of media elements with central figures from the music industry echo the earlier life cycles of superstar performers Elvis Presley and The Beatles. Choi and Maliangkay (2014) emphasize how K-pop's transnational elements are based on international collaborations like the Korean-Indonesia talent agency YS Media Entertainment. As a result of its impressive fandom, K-pop is widely considered to have amplified South Korea's soft power (Kim, 2016).

Gathering and Stanning

Music tends to inspire people to gather around it, and being a music fan today often involves participating in a community, whether online or at live events. These communities provide a space for fans to share their enthusiasm, create content, discuss interpretations of lyrics, and celebrate the artist's work collectively. As fans find one another, their fascination with musicians and music means that they share a common language, reference points, and insider knowledge that express a shared love for the music and also the perceived values and meanings it and the artists express.

Like sports fandom, pop music fans frequently engage in competitive behaviors, comparing chart positions, streaming numbers, and award wins, much like sports fans compare and take pride in sports statistics. The members of music fandoms today do not simply express their support for their favorite artists. Instead, they actively participate in various campaigns to boost chart positions, music sales, stream counts, and the metrics that measure the strength of an artist's social media power. They vote in polls, organize and participate in fan events, and mobilize around social media campaigns related to the artist. In effect, fans become an unpaid promotional and public relations labor force. Although often such fan-celebrity relationships are described as "para-social" (Horton and Wohl, 1956), a more thorough investigation will reveal that the relationships are very often actually bidirectional.

Nancy Baym (2018), a fandom scholar whose research on soap opera and music fans dates back to the same transitional period which produced *Textual Poachers*, recently described the relationships between musical performers and fans, stressing the messy human relationships which emerge as an outgrowth of what she calls relational labor, and calling on fans to recognize the personal boundaries and emotional needs of the idols they stan:

> "We also need to remember that people's work is entangled in people's selves, and when we engage them as professionals, we also engage them as humans, with all their foibles and vulnerabilities. Being the center of attention does not come with an infinite ability to absorb the relational demands of others. It is always appropriate to be kind. Remember that just finding a public persona interesting does not mean that you are entitled to a person's time, let alone their private life. Just as we want others to respect our autonomy, we need to respect theirs. We must also quit stalking people and heaping abuse upon them just because it's easy. Even virtual slings and arrows cause real suffering." (P. 202)

Beyond following the object of their fandom, fans may also engage in broader cultural or social issues promoted or represented by their favorite artists, athletes, or authors. Music fandoms may include participating in charitable causes supported by the artist and advocating for social justice issues touched upon in their music. For example, KPOP4PLANET is a collective of K-Pop fan groups who have combined efforts to advocate for climate action, focusing on initiatives that include promoting sustainable concerts, supporting reforestation projects, and urging K-Pop idols to speak out about environmental issues. Traditionally, music has been a powerful voice for social movements. It is consistent with this heritage that music fandoms today also engage in social and political activism, often mobilized by the artists themselves or by the community's consensus on the importance of certain issues. **Fan Activism** is considered another example of K-Pop-based activism, in this case, related to BTS and Black Lives Matter.

Although likely much rarer than media depictions suggest, music fandom is no stranger to the culture of "stanning." The term itself is derived from Eminem's song "Stan," a fictional tale about an obsessive fan who ends up committing suicide and killing his girlfriend after the object of his fandom fails to answer his fan mail. And, as one would expect in a toxic culture that has spread its toxicity to online culture, we find fandoms (for musicians, celebrities, actors and athletes) can sometimes lead to unsavory behaviors, even taunting those who have recently gone through tragedy (Mercier, 2022). Although certainly not the norm, these behaviors may include trolling, harassment of other fans or critics, and intense online battles that may mirror the divisive nature of political partisanship.

We are intrigued by recent phenomena like "Ethical Stanning" in fandoms that seem to especially include music fandoms. "Ethical Stanning" refers to the practice of supporting celebrities and public figures based not only on their popularity or talent but also on how well they align with ethical values and social justice issues. Members of fandoms will engage in discussions and critiques about their favorite celebrities' actions, behaviors, and endorsements. They will subsequently hold them accountable for problematic or harmful acts. For example, fans online are engaged in discussions about whether or not Taylor Swift is an "ethical billionaire" or whether she has merely used the language of vulnerability and empowerment to enrich herself. Ethical Stanning seems like an important phenomenon that suggests a shift in the traditional power imbalance between fans and celebrities, facilitated by the rapid spread of information and discussion over social media and the response of the entertainment industry to these moral discourses.

CHAPTER 8:

Fandoms in Action: Media, Consumption, and Serious Leisure

iterary fandoms and their media outcroppings presented the world with some of the earliest examples of fandom, such as when Arthur Conan Doyle killed Sherlock Holmes in 1893, and fans (who called themselves "Sherlockians") held public demonstrations of mourning and later began writing their own richly detailed fan fiction using Doyle's characters (Stein and Busse, 2012). When we look at contemporary fandoms and fanfic, such as the *50 Shades of Gray* fandom, which evolved from *Twilight* fandom and fanfic, we can discern within them the history of past fandoms and their actions.

Alexandra Edwards (2023) has called attention to what she calls the "fandom creation myth": "Western media fandom, this myth tells us, might have gained popularity in the 1960s and 1970s as female audiences mimeographed and mailed each other *Star Trek* fanzines, but it owes its creation to the male-dominated world of the 1930s science fiction pulps. A version of fan history that celebrates men as original founders ignores the rich fan cultures of the early twentieth century, and it erases the many women writers, readers, and film fans who transformed American culture by their participation in early forms of fandom." (p. 2)—not to mention the many female fans who propelled Lisztomania into history. The broader our understanding of the scope of fandom in the present, the clearer it becomes that our explanation requires multiple origins and histories. The one Edwards (2023) traces goes through small magazines in the early 20th century that published debates amongst women as well as original fiction and fiction written in response to other writers.

Another history of fandom might take us to the late 19th century and the emergence of so-called "Matinee girls," that is, young women who regularly attended plays not so much to admire the work of the era's great playwrights but rather to enjoy the pleasures of being free to admire the performers and gaze upon the male body. Such conduct was deemed inappropriate at a point when theater was struggling to gain high art status after pop culture origins in the Anglo-American world and as directors were seeking to create unified stage effects rather than call attention to the virtuosity of individual players (Ehler, 2018; Mendonca, 2018). Journalist Arthur Symons (1865-1945) debated in the *New Review*: "If the female figure is supposed to be indecent, why is not the male figure indecent also? We are assured that the 'baser passions' of the male part of an audience are likely to be 'inflamed' by the sight of the outline of the female figure. Are the 'baser passions' then of the female audience likely to be inflamed by the sight of the outline of the male figure?" (As quoted in Ehlert). The pleasures of the female fan—then as now—were the subject of some scandal, because they represented a different relationship to the medium than that prescribed by the male critics. The women not only took pleasure in looking but they also expressed their pleasure during the performance and afterwards, giving them a voice from which to speak beyond the narrow confines of the sexual roles prescribed for them in late Victorian culture.

We might understand the emergence of film stardom over the first few decades of the 20th century as an extension of the Matinee Girl phenomenon. In early cinema, actors were generally not identified by name in the film's credits, yet audiences soon developed preferences for particular performers and gave them nicknames so they could discuss them with each other. For example, Mary Pickford was initially known simply as "the girl with the curls." In her history of early filmgoing, Katherine Fuller-Seeley (1996) argues that as the studio system took shape, there was a deep appreciation of the roles film stars played in drawing female fans into the theaters and a wealth of publication emerged to fuel these fans' desires for more information about these vivid screen personalities.

The nature of female-centered film fandom hit a crisis point in the 1926 death and funeral of Rudolf Valentino. Valentino, then only 36, was one of the most desired male performers of the American silent cinema, with a massive female following. It has been estimated that more than 100,000 fans, mostly women, tried to attend his final rites, resulting in a riot as they struggled to get a glimpse of his body and, in some accounts, ghoulishly ripped his clothing off for one final souvenir. This fan behavior was only one part of the histrionics as his former lover, Pola Negri, fainted onto his lowering casket, an act many felt was a publicity stunt, suggesting the close relationship between fandom and promotion went back to the 1920s, at least.

Another historian, Diana Anselmo (2019), tells us, "In the early twentieth century, the leisure activities recommended to schoolgirls clustered around reading, handcrafts, and life-writing (i.e., correspondence and journaling), entertainments that privileged the mind and the home over the body and the public. Original movie-fan practices followed in this tradition, taking two principal forms: scrapbooking and letter-writing, followed closely by illustrated journaling." Historians today are finding these women's scrapbooks valuable resources for reconstructing the nature of these early fan cultures. For example, Chad Dell (2006) has used scrapbooks and newsletters to reclaim the history of female wrestling fans in the early television era of the 1940s and 1950s. Fuller-Seeley identifies a second fan culture, more closely but not exclusively associated with men, who would participate in scenario writing contests hosted by movie magazines, make their own amateur films inspired by cinematic genres, and otherwise seek entry into the entertainment industry. From the start, then, movie fandom was gendered and incorporated a wide array of different forms of personal and collective expression,

Today, fans of media franchises such as Doctor Who, Star Trek, Star Wars, Lord of the Rings, Marvel, and Harry Potter are faced not only with a rich and complex set of media and literary texts encompassing panoplies of both commercially manufactured and fan-made productions but also generational shifts and sociocultural adaptations of these stories and their characters. We will discuss the models of fandom, spectatorship and authorship that inform today's transmedia storytelling in **Fandom as Audience**. These models remain implicitly and explicitly gendered with the media industry imagining its audience as largely white men, even if the reality differs considerably from those assumptions.

Mel Stanfill (2018) rightly points out that, historically, race has not been actively engaged within these media franchises. "In the media fandoms that fan studies tends to focus on, which I'll call Predominantly White Fandoms, engagement with race is ... present but not prevalent" (p. 306). Newer offerings of these franchises have all incorporated greater diversity of characters, particularly evident in featuring Black main characters and the presence of LGBTQ+ characters (in the Star Trek series). The introduction of these new elements speaks to entertainment company's attempts to broaden global and local audiences and make the shows more appealing.

Like sports and music fans, members of media fandoms are active participants who see their identities reflected (or not) in the media they consume. For example, the recent casting of Ncuti Gatwa, a queer Black man, as the Doctor has been a point of celebration for some, representing a broader trend toward inclusivity in media. This shift has been seen as a crucial counterpoint to challenge what was often inaccurately seen as the traditional white and male-dominated demographics of earlier fandom eras. The Doctor's sexuality has long been a point of speculation, sometimes read as asexual because he often avoids any sexual entanglements, and sometimes as heterosexual because the River Song storyline implies a future marriage, but with the casting of Gatwa (best known previously to British audiences for his portrayal of a flamboyant and openly gay character of British-Nigerian descent on *Sex Education*) the series began to explore the possibility of same-sex relationships, especially through a same-sex kiss in "Rogue.".

Modern fandom is characterized by a critical and creative engagement with the media. In a related vein, Alfred L Martin, Jr. (2019) investigates the complex and interconnected discourses within black fandom through an analysis of 50 interviews with black individuals about their views on Tyler Perry's media works, the blockbuster film Black Panther, and the African American ballerina Misty Copeland. His research reveals four key themes that shape black fandom. The first theme, "must-see blackness," reflects a sense of civic responsibility among black fans to support and engage with black cultural representations in all forms. This is closely tied to the second theme, economic consumption, where fans are aware of the fragile presence of blackness in predominantly white or historically hostile spaces and, thus, feel compelled to financially support black media and figures to ensure their continued visibility and success. The third theme centers on the educational and role-modeling potential of these fan objects, where the worthiness of a figure or work is evaluated based on its capacity to teach and inspire. Finally, these themes—pedagogical value, economic consumption, and must-see blackness—are interwoven, highlighting how black fans are acutely aware of and respond to the strategies and influences of cultural industries. This awareness shapes their fandom and anti-fandom.

Media fandom is also a vibrant and multifaceted phenomenon that involves transmedia narratives, media-induced tourism, and participatory culture. Fandom transcends single mediums, as fans engage across platforms—creating, discussing, and sharing content that keeps the narratives alive well beyond their original format and constantly builds them into new forms. The rise of social media has amplified this, with discussions about episodes, new seasons, and related content becoming crucial parts of the fan experience. Series like Star Trek and *Game of Thrones* exemplify how fandom can resurrect or sustain shows. And fan-driven events like Oscar watch parties, themed food preps, and other rituals add rich new layers of communal engagement to the media fandom experience. Moreover, the shift from traditional theaters and TV to streaming/on-demand services has transformed how fans interact with these media, offering new ways to access, binge, and discuss their favorite content. Fans lining up for cameos or immersive experiences involving their favorite shows underscore the active, participatory nature of modern fandom, marking it as one of the most dynamic forces in contemporary consumer culture.

Different models of fanship and fandom have taken root in different national contexts and in relation to distinctive media industries. Aswin Punthabaker (2007), for example, has described the "public" nature of filmgoing in India, suggesting that the aesthetics of Bollywood are star-centered and often involve playful breaking of the fourth wall so as to directly address the film fans in the house. The cinema hall allows Indian fans to address the movie, collectively and individually, in real-time through a range of call and response practices, "whistling and commenting loudly, throwing flowers, coins, or ribbons when the star first appears on the screen, singing along and dancing in the aisles" (p. 293).

Punthabaker argues that this participatory dimension, which many have seen as central to Indian filmgoing, must be understood as part of a continuum of other Zones of Engagement that are woven deep into the everyday practices of this culture: "Yes, there are rowdies and *rasikas*. However, denying the existence of several other sites and modes of participation and continuing to relegate fan activity to the fringes of a transnational public culture shaped so strongly by cinema will not only sustain cultural hierarchies but will also mean turning a blind eye to the many important ways in which cultural and political identities are being shaped in "new" media spaces today" (p. 294). Conversations begun in the picture house may spill over into the streets or local cafes and coffee houses. Indian fans are especially drawn to the music contained in Bollywood's flamboyant song sequences, often listening to the songs many times on soundtrack albums before they see the film so they can singalong and incorporating the songs into a range of everyday performance situations. Sangita Shresthsova (2011), who was like Punthabaker part of an exceptional cohort of graduate students Henry taught at MIT, has also traced the ways local culture clubs around the world and student groups on campus mastered the dance numbers and improvised and staged their own interpretations of the songs within their own contexts. Punthabaker's account of Indian film fandom extends to the online world where networked fans in India and across the diaspora share files, discuss musical scores, support composers, and otherwise use their fandom to promote greater awareness of someone like composer A.R. Rahman and not simply the stars and celebrities in front of the camera.

Media and literary fans may feel powerful connections to the storyline and characters, experiencing real emotions as they follow the adventures of the objects of their fandom. Just as sports fans live through the highs and lows of their teams' performances, so do the perceived outcomes of narrative and character arcs affect the mood and emotional state of media fans. Like sports and music fans, being a media fan today often involves engaging with an offline and online community. Many fans gather to watch episodes together, creating a shared experience. Sports fans critique coaching and trade decisions, while music fans question song and fashion choices. Similarly, media fans analyze and critique developments like changes in showrunners, the influence of large corporations, and the evolution of show themes and tones. There is also a strong element of nostalgia, as seen in the references to past episodes and the historical significance of the show for individuals.

Consumption-related Fandoms

What does it mean to be a die-hard fan?, we might wonder. The sociologist Jenny Huberman studied a US company called Eternal Image, which, in 2006, became one of the first public companies in the United States to offer licensed-brand funerary products. Some of the company's most popular product lines resulted from 'die-hard' fans who desired to take their passionate interest in baseball teams, Star Trek, and even the rock band KISS with them to the grave. Among the participants, Huberman interviewed for her article was a funeral director, "Jonathan Wheatley, who was tasked with organizing the memorial service for a life-long Harley Davidson enthusiast:

> I want to tell you about a service that we had for an individual who really wanted to memorialize himself and for his family to create a lasting memory for them. And he was a Harley Davidson Rider, loved his Harley, Amen.

And he wanted his Harley to be with him, during his celebration of life, and so we had his casket there, in the chapel, his Harley was parked right in front of the casket, all of his Harley Riders were there, we had special seating for them, of course, they filled up the majority of our chapel, and uh, at the end of the service when we were going to the cemetery, everyone left the chapel, walked outside, and there was a Harley Hearse, waiting to carry him to the cemetery. So this gentlemen was placed in the back of his Harley Hearse, his wife was on her Harley behind the hearse, and all of his buddies, there were Hogs for days. Hundreds of Hogs, it was a great experience, his family had a memory that they will carry with them for the rest of their life. They will always remember that their father, their husband loved his Harley and instilled in them to continue riding" (Huberman, 2012, pp. 476-7).

What are we to make of this form of fandom, which centers on a brand of motorcycle? It is a form of passionate engagement with a fan object, shared in a collective with others. We consider it as another form of fandom, akin to sports and music fandom in its fervor but unique in its manifestations and cultural positioning. However, as with the presence of the Harley Davidsons at the funeral, this type of fandom tends to foreground the role of materiality. The materiality of fandom manifests in the way in which physical objects–and, if we extend materiality to digital materialities, as Paul Leonardi (2010) suggests we do, to digital artifacts– serve as embodiments of fan identities, desires, and social relations. Drawing on Daniel Miller's theories (see Borgerson 2014), the materiality of fandom is not just about the physical presence of objects but how these objects mediate and shape the social experiences of fandom. In fandom, material artifacts—such as t-shirts, baseball caps, collectibles, books, and professional and fan art—are imbued with layers of emotional and symbolic significance, nostalgia and intertextuality, craftsmanship and collectability; they serve as vessels for personal and collective memory. These objects materialize fandom. Through them, abstract affiliations are made concrete, allowing fans to navigate their identities and social networks through the tangible expression of cultural consumption and production.

Motorcycles are certainly not the only vehicles that inspire such deep and abiding passion. Every Friday throughout the summer, Rob's neighborhood in Los Angeles is treated to a vintage car show in a local parking lot. Car fans from miles around drive their classic cars, many of them American muscle cars—Mustangs, Corvettes, Challengers, GTOs and Camaros—but also many classic cars like Rivieras, Thunderbirds, and Bel Airs, even a few working Model T's, to the parking lot, set up lawn chairs, and then spend the afternoon circulating, admiring, and talking about their cars. Some of them set up signs that describe the car, its history, how they found it, its engine and speed specifications, the work they've done on it, and so on. There is live music and vendors, and a few of the cars are usually for sale. The atmosphere is a lot like a comic book convention, except that these are fans of classic cars and this gathering is their fandom.

Many of these car enthusiasts restore and customize their vehicles (and other people's, too), turning each car into a canvas that reflects their personal style, creativity, skill, and engineering prowess. Library and Information Science researchers Annemaree Lloyd and Michael Olsson (2019) write about the community of car restorers, noting how this collective is bound within discourses of loyalty to the practice of restoration, to the material object of cars, and to narratives of expertise, maintenance, and preservation. Their findings also demonstrate that "car restorers, along with other serious leisure communities, have become the unacknowledged custodians of a large body of hands-on knowledge that would otherwise be in danger of being lost in an increasingly post-industrial world" (p. 1033).

The notion that these fan groups may be custodians of knowledge that would otherwise be forgotten draws our attention to their social importance. Again, the evidence demonstrates that these are not mere materialist "consumers" or duped collectors, but people who find fulfillment engaging in socially important tasks, which, as we will explain below, relate to the concept of "serious leisure" (Stebbins, 1982).

Consider those who practice salsa dancing. The energetic and exciting dance style with roots in Afro-Caribbean traditions from Cuba and Puerto Rico, has spread globally, including to many South American countries like Brazil. It flourishes in diverse settings, such as nightclubs, dance studios, festivals, and informal gatherings, where enthusiasts unite to celebrate their shared passion. Salsa is an immersive cultural experience that demands dedication to mastering its complicated steps, musicality, and ever-changing partner dynamics (Hewer and Hamilton, 2010). The deep, sustained commitment and collective engagement required for salsa mean that it functions as a form of fandom, where dancers are not merely participants but fans of the dance, its history, and its culture. The salsa community, with its shared values, rituals, and collective events, mirrors the dynamics of fandom, fostering a collective identity centered on the love of dance. In Brazil and beyond, salsa is part of the cultural fabric, inspiring fan-like devotion that enriches the lives of its practitioners.

As the Harley-Davidson and salsa dancing examples indicate, consumption or brand-based fandoms encompass a wide range of activities. Recognizing this fact creates an urgent impetus to include these consumer-oriented passions within fandom studies. We embrace that important challenge. In this short section, we delve into some of the characteristics of this type of fandom, in which collection and consumption transcend mere hobbies, impacting the lives of their enthusiasts significantly. We can often find the joy of creation and the expression of imagination at the heart of these playful consumption-related fandoms. For instance, adult Fans of LEGO (AFOL) exemplify this through their sophisticated designs and constructions, known as My Own Creations (MOCs). These creations are not just personal projects but are often shared within communities, celebrated at conventions, or even sold, turning a passion into a profession (Hains and Mazzarella, 2019)..

Like media fans, consumption enthusiasts gather in groups that affirm and reinforce their shared identities through various activities. These gatherings, whether local clubs, online forums, or international conventions, serve as hubs for sharing knowledge, trading tips, and fostering friendships. The sense of belonging is palpable as members unite over their shared passions, from board games and pinball machines to amusement parks, Barbie dolls, and rare coins.

Some consumption-related fandoms feature collecting not merely as a hobby but as a lifestyle that involves meticulous research,

ADULT FANS

The term "adult fans" often implies that something is surprising or even shocking about adults continuing to play and engage with popular fandom past childhood. "Adult Fans," though, is most often deployed to stigmatize adults as surplus audiences for children's media and activities. (We discuss surplus audiences more fully in **Fandom as Audience**). Much, for example, has been written about the "Bronies," the adult and mostly male (and often queer) fans of *My Little Pony*. These fans of an animated series designed primarily for young girls have been depicted as "perverse" because it has transgressed so many assumptions about the intended market for the franchise (Hunting and Hains, 2022)

Yet, as the Adult Fans of Lego example suggests, and as we also discuss in **Fandom as Co-Creation**, there is an expanding market for toys, games, and playful experiences that primarily, if not exclusively, target adults. In the case of Lego, adult fans host their own conventions, are the focus of corporate marketing and products, and have become the focus of the reality television series, *Lego Masters*. Initiatives to include diverse groups, such as Adult Female Fans of LEGO (AFFOL) or Gay Fans of LEGO (GayFOL), highlight the progressive nature of these communities, networking, and sometimes significant financial investment. For some collectors, there are thrills in hunting and acquiring rare items, which may appreciate in value over time. For example, Donald Case (2009) writes that just about every American city with a population of over 100,000 people has a local coin-collecting (numismatic) club, and many smaller communities do as well. There are frequent coin shows, which Case considers to be halfway between formal and informal arrangements and somewhere between the economic and the festive. After conducting a participant-observation study of a coin collecting community, Case finds that "they are motivated by the potential for self-development, social interactions with other collectors, and financial gains, and at times by compulsive collecting" (p. 729). For some, their collections are priceless links to times and identities with which they never intend to part. For others, they are an investment vehicle or an enjoyable way to spend time and meet other people. Members of these groups find a sense of belonging, conversation, and community.

striving to ensure that everyone can share in the joy and camaraderie that these activities provide. In China and across much of Asia, the entrepreneurial success of Pop Mart, discussed in **Locations of Fandom**, has rested on a core market of 20-30 year-old women, much as young adult men have been the primary drivers of the specialized action figure market in the United States.

Rebecca Williams (2021) has written about the intense ridicule that has been directed against Adult Disney fans as well as the central role these more mature consumers (as family members, as couples, as fans) have played in extending the market for their theme parks; Disney targets such consumers through their specialized publication and fan conventions under the D23 banner. Through such practices and others, Disney has increasingly become a lifestyle and even a fashion brand for adults. We can see this shift of products initially aimed primarily at children reaching adult consumers as part of the logic of surplus consumption, discussed in **Fandom as Audience**.

Disney and other theme parks have increasingly catered to adult visitors by enhancing their offerings beyond traditional family-friendly attractions. At Epcot, for instance, the World Showcase has become a hub for adult-oriented experiences, featuring international cuisine that appeals to sophisticated palates, with restaurants like Le Cellier Steakhouse in Canada and the Chefs de France in the France Pavilion. The introduction of events like the Epcot International Food & Wine Festival has further expanded the appeal by offering a wide variety of gourmet food and beverages from around the world, including craft beers, fine wines, and specialty cocktails. Disney has also embraced the trend of mixology with themed bars like Oga's Cantina in *Star Wars: Galaxy's Edge* at Disney's Hollywood Studios, where adults can enjoy unique, Star Wars themed drinks like the Jedi Mind Trick or the Dagobah Slug Slinger in an immersive environment. Shopping has also seen a shift, with high-end boutiques offering designer goods and exclusive merchandise that caters to adult tastes. Kate Spade now has a Disney collection, and Pandora offers Disney and Marvel lines. These enhancements reflect broader trends in Disney merchandising and theme park development, recognizing that adult fans are a significant part of their audience and offering them a broader menu of adult-sized and indulgent experiences. Here, adult fans, far from stigmatized for their childish tastes, have emerged as a desired market with greater disposable income than children and the offerings have been adjusted for their more mature tastes.

Fandoms as Serious Leisure

These activities are recognizable as "serious leisure," a concept coined in the 1980s by sociologist Robert Stebbins to refer to the way people increasingly turn to the world of leisure activities to provide them with the satisfaction that they do not find through their work lives. Stebbins (1982, p. 251) contends that, in post-industrial society, people increasingly turn to leisure pursuits in order to "express their abilities, fulfill their potential, and identify themselves as unique humans." As well, they may find a sense of community. Stebbins describes three types of serious leisure: (1) amateurism, in which activities are transformed into serious, committed avocations that serve publics; (2) hobbyist pursuits, which are specialized pursuits that the hobbyist finds interesting and enjoys doing because of their durable benefits (hobbyists include collectors, makers, activity participants, and players), and (3) career volunteering, a voluntary action involving helping activities that can be deemed beneficial. Summarizing his perspective on the personal and social value of serious leisure, Stebbins quotes Cicero:

"If the soul has food for study and learning, nothing is more delightful than an old age of leisure. .... Leisure consists in all those virtuous activities by which a man grows morally, intellectually, and spiritually. It is that which makes life worth living" (p. 268).

Studies of serious leisure pursuits have included the following activities: birdwatching, photography, gardening, model railroading, amateur astronomy, genealogy research, amateur dramatics (theater), playing musical instruments, volunteering for charitable organizations, amateur sports, crafting, collecting, writing, amateur radio, dance, chess playing, historical reenactment, fishing, hiking and mountaineering, wine making, and many others. There are very clear overlaps with other types of fandoms. As the participatory culture concept does, serious leisure draws our attention to these activities' educational and social benefits. Building models, solving puzzles, exploring the history and geography of stamps and coins, or engaging in strategic gameplay can provide relief from the stresses of daily life, but they can also provide safe spaces for people in which they can gather, experiment, and learn.

Just as consumer culture is (usually, but with exceptions) an inclusive space, the inclusivity of consumption-oriented fandoms is also noteworthy, with many of these groups welcoming members across age, gender, and cultural spectrums. Much like music, sports, or media fandoms, consumption-oriented fandoms define personal and community narratives, linking individuals to broader cultural or national heritages. For instance, Harley-Davidson enthusiasts often see their involvement as tied to a spirit of freedom and American identity. For their participants, these rich experiences are as multifaceted and integrated into the lives of their participants as other forms of fandom. All of these rich varieties of fandom have their own rituals and emotional cycles, providing their own unique rhythms and experiences, enriching the lives of those who partake in them. In the next chapter, we continue to stretch the concept of fans and fandoms a bit further.

CHAPTER 9:
Extending the Frame

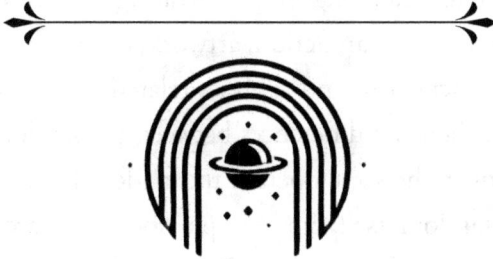

Life is full of joys, paradoxes, complexity, and tensions. Cycles of growth and decay, happiness and despair, etch psychic rings in us as the years pass. One of the greatest joys we know as a people, as human beings, is to use these common experiences to produce, enjoy, and share songs and stories, to follow old and ongoing tales, to find ourselves lost inside the telling of some story, and to share that experience with others.

Considering the various types of fandoms we have explored—of sports, music, media, and consumption activities and brands—we must notice the large degrees of overlap in the ways these groups express their enthusiasm, interact with their passion, and contribute to a community, albeit in different contexts and through various mediums. In every case, there are consequential emotional investments between fans and the object of their fandom. This could be the thrill of a live sports game, the attachment to characters and narratives in a television series, the emotional resonance of a favorite music track, or the ludic excitement of a role-playing game. Each shapes its members' personal identity and is expressed in various ways, such as wearing a t-shirt or other apparel, using images in a social media profile, in conversation, or in other ways they represent themselves to the world. All of these types of fandoms create communities that often extend globally. These communities are formed around shared interests and passions, with fans interacting through online forums, social media, fan conventions, and live events. And, across all types of fandoms, we find fans engaging in creating content related to their interests. This includes fan fiction, artwork, cover songs, fan theories, and extensive discussions and analyses related to their passions.

Of course, there are differences between the fandoms as well, but these relate more to how members of the fandom interact with content than with the fandom itself. For example, sports fans are often engaged in real-time events and experiences. Their fandom revolves around live games, seasons, and the real-world achievements of athletes and teams. Music fans interact with art that is both a personal and shared experience. Music listening can be an individual activity and a communal one at concerts or social gatherings. Media fans interact with narrative-driven content, focusing on story arcs, character development, and speculative fiction. Their engagement is often episodic, following the show's releases and narrative developments. Consumption-oriented fandoms revolve around the ludic, interactive, and sometimes collectible nature of their interests. Fans engage by playing, building, collecting, or customizing their consumption experiences, whether through constructing model kits, gathering rare items, or participating in games that require strategic thinking and creativity. This type of fandom not only celebrates the products themselves but also fosters a community of enthusiasts who share tips and trade items and gather at events to celebrate their passions together.

Fandoms are vibrant cultures of passionate engagement through which individuals or groups celebrate, support, critique, reimagine, and derive pleasure from interest in and activity related to a focal fan object. As we have seen in this analysis, fandom includes forming communities around a wide variety of shared passions and fascinations for objects of fandom, whether those objects involve sports, music, television series, theme parks, video games, board games, brands, car restoration, birdwatching, or other types of hobbies. Fans express their enthusiasm through activities such as attending, audiencing, collecting, creating, discussing, or participating in events related to their interests. The essence of fandom lies in the emotional connection fans develop with their interests and with each other, fostering a sense of identity, community, and often, a form of creative or critical engagement.

Although these emotional connections are serious, the passions they are rooted in are interrelated with the realms of leisure and consumption. One cannot, for example, be a "fan" of one's own family or ethnicity. When one is a major fan of one's own country, we call this patriotism, not fandom, though as we discuss in **Fandom as Public,** the two are increasingly intertwined in ways we do not yet fully understand. Likewise, as we explore in the **Fandom as Devotion**, devotees of religion are adherents of that religion, not fans of it. Although there are some levels of interesting overlap, we believe that there are clear boundaries demarcating fandom from other passionate pursuits, just as there are for all meaningful social categories. We will be looking in great depth, and from many angles, at many of these principles and differences, and sometimes at their overlaps with other categories like family, religion, and nationalism, as we examine the various frames through which we can understand the vast and dynamic world of fandom.

Broadening the Concept of Fandom

Our discussion of fandom extends beyond media consumption and their narrative world-building storytelling forms to brands and gameplay. We are talking in a wider sense about how grassroots participatory cultures emerge and operate in relation to their own passion for particular kinds of cultural phenomena and elements that have an "official" or "for-profit" type of interest that runs alongside the moral/gift economy and "unofficial" ethos and structures of fandom. In other words, the phenomenon is centered on passionate grassroots organization, investigation, and/or creativity around certain aspects of the human experience, whatever those might be. For a long time, particular kinds of experience have been associated with sports, entertainment, and religion, but it is not the experience but the passionate response to it that we hold to be central to the conception of a "fandom." Fandoms are types of collective expressions that have wide currency globally and topically.

We also have to recognize Henry's concept of participatory culture, which is the focus of its own book, **Fandom as Participatory Culture.** The concept of participatory culture extends beyond fandom to describe a range of other cultural communities and practices—crafters, bloggers, videomakers, gamers, makers, and so forth—who actively participate in acts of creation and circulation around their shared interests, who learn from their engagement with each other, and who socially organize into networks to promote their common interests, forging communities that are not necessarily geographically rooted but may reflect their desire for affiliation with like-minded others. However, as the following five border cases of UFO enthusiasts, foodies, Steampunks, amateur adult entertainment creators, and followers of strongman-type politicians, attest, the lines between fandom and other forms of participatory culture are blurry at best.

UFO Enthusiasts

The UFO community, with its rich history and intriguing present, exhibits all of the core characteristics of a participatory culture and mirrors the enthusiastic engagement seen in many types of fandoms. The fascination with UFOs gained significant traction during and after World War II, following numerous mysterious sightings by military personnel. These historical accounts helped shape a culture that expertly blends scientific curiosity with the thrill of uncovering the unknown, forming a foundation that supports scholarly, speculative, and even spiritual pursuits and that spans from casual interest to rigorous investigation. Members of this community participate in a wide array of activities that reflect typical fandom behaviors. They gather at conferences, engage in online forums, and produce diverse content ranging from documentaries to speculative articles. Organizations like the Mutual UFO Network (MUFON) provide structured environments for these activities, but their presence is broad across social media. Members consume and create content, from analyzing mainstream media coverage of UFOs to generating independent reports and theories. This interaction with media is twofold: it helps shape community perceptions and serves as a platform for alternative narratives, often in response to official reports that community members' may view with skepticism.

The UFO community's relationship with official narratives is particularly noteworthy. Its persistent skepticism towards government and institutional reports leads to the production of alternative accounts and theories. This skepticism is a binding force that unites the community against perceived opacity from official sources. Fandom Studies research can help explain some aspects of this phenomenon, especially the mastery of lore and the production of alternative accounts that closely mirror those of fan theory.

Formal gatherings like Contact in the Desert and the Roswell UFO Festival serve as critical social gatherings where enthusiasts strengthen their shared identities and exchange knowledge. The community's engagement is global and local. While international networks foster broad discussions and theories, local chapters focus on region-specific phenomena and engage in activities like local sky-watches and community meetings.

Finally, the pervasive portrayal of UFOs in popular culture—films, television, and literature—not only reflects but also amplifies the community's widespread influence, as their speculative and investigative narratives are increasingly incorporated into broader cultural discussions. Through these various dimensions, the UFO community provides us with a clear example of a dynamic and participatory culture that thrives on its members' social and investigative engagements. Much as the members of a sports, music, or media fandom do, UFO enthusiasts partake in a vibrant culture of passionate engagement through which they celebrate, support, critique, reimagine, and derive pleasure from their interest in UFOs and activities related to them.

Foodies

Over the past several decades, there has been a growing popular interest in "celebrity chefs," who are seen as rivals competing to dominate the "food world." Some argue that such marketing and self-branding have shifted traditional gourmets' focus on the dishes themselves (which may or may not constitute a fandom, more of a consumer network perhaps; see Rob's discussion of coffee enthusiasts in **Fandom as Technoculture**.) The new focus on the chef's personality and style becomes more clearly a fandom, operating according to many of the same principles as other celebrity-driven fan cultures, a shift that has become more empathic as more and more celebrity chefs have developed their own reality television series. Such series may run from cooking competitions (*Iron Chef, Master Chef, Top Chef*), where they serve as judges and mentors of emerging talent, to travel shows (*Parts Unknown, Taste the Nation*), where they learn and teach about the history and culture of food within different culinary traditions.

In *Food TV*, Tasha Oren (2023) traces the evolution of the genre from Betty Crocker on radio through Julia Child on television to the current moment where a proliferating range of formats are designed to construct and extend the reign of the celebrity chef. She has this to say about one iconic program: "*Chef's Table* would decisively reconfigure professional cooking from fine craft to art and offer the chef's creative process as artistic biography, exalted human drama, and peak experience recounted on an operatic scale. This narrative framing of individual vision, born of biography and honed through monumental and principled struggle, marked a summit of sort for the figure of the chef as TV subject." (89)

Oren describes Food TV as having a pedagogical goal, helping people learn more about food and encouraging them to try new cooking practices in their everyday lives (initially). The rise of celebrity chefs has resulted in more virtuoso forms of food preparation, which are beyond the skill set of the everyday "home cook," though the existence of this category suggests the way food television often centers on the transition from amateur to professional. These reality shows market kits for home preparation, classes and performances that tour the country, and many other forms of fan participation. Anecdotally, we also know of people who construct food challenges for their children as a way of enlivening their family interactions, mimicking the format through their own everyday practices.

With *The Bear*, FX/ Hulu's acclaimed television "dramedy" (drama-comedy), the focus is on the creation of a new upscale restaurant in Chicago, which gives the producers ample excuse to stage scenes at famous eateries and also to include cameos by celebrity chefs such as Joyce Chiu, Daniel Boulud, Paulie James, and Christina Tosi, among others. Whatever value these performers contribute to the story development or in anchoring the realism of this series as the fictional chef protagonist engages with his world peers, such "stunt casting" constitutes a classic crossover marketing technique designed to expand their audience. These chefs' presence may attract foodies who follow their careers and gain free press in publications such as *Food & Wine* which service foodie culture. Many foodies already watch the show – because of its narrative focus, but this approach also draws in folks who are primarily following the celebrity of particular chefs.

These celebrity chefs are frequently (but not always) young and traditionally attractive. They tend to have vivid personalities, which they have honed through their appearances as "food stars" on a variety of programs and other public-facing activities before they host their own programs, The archetypes for these celebrity chefs might be Anthony Bourdain, who was the focus of an acclaimed posthumous documentary, *The Roadrunner,* but who wrote best-selling books, starred in multiple television series, and otherwise developed a status as a personality that rivaled or exceeded that of his food preparation skills. His logical successor may be Gordon Ramsey, probably best known for his hosting role on *Master Chef* but so much more. Founded in 1997, his restaurant group has been awarded 17 Michelin Stars. Ramsay's status as a television star initially centered around his fiery temper and profanity spewing (both initially read alongside the release of a series of best-selling books showing the behind-the-scenes of the restaurant industry and stressing the stress of the job of being a chef). The names of some of his earlier programs, such as *Boiling Point, Hell's Kitchen, Ramsay's Kitchen Nightmares, and The F Word,* allude to this early persona. Ramsay still occasionally evokes this initial reputation when he chews out contestants on *Master Chef* or throws their dishes against the wall in contempt. Still, through the years, his image has softened, and he has become more family-friendly, as seen on *Master Chef Junior*, or supportive, as seen on *Next Level Chef.*

The Ramsay's—the chef, his wife, and their children—also became the focus of their own behind-the-scenes web series (*Matilda and the*

Ramsay Clan) which showed how their everyday lives were also centered around food and cooking. This show has also been part of an effort to develop his oldest daughter, Matilda, into a food celebrity in her own right. The fact that his loyal fan base will follow him wherever he goes and try out any new Gordon Ramsay venture, such as his food travel series *Gordon's Great Escape,* has meant that he could sustain a media empire, with one series starting as soon as the season of another wraps. During this same time, he shifted between American and British television. He has also directed his celebrity status towards various public causes, including focusing on the low quality of food served in prisons and schools. A sign at one of his chains of restaurants, depicted in a photo in Figure 9.1 that was taken in Seoul, suggests how recognizable his visage and his personality have become worldwide.

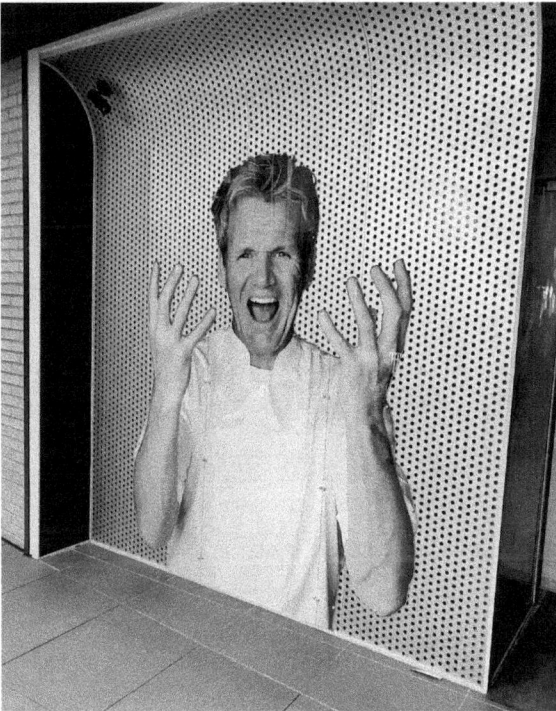

Figure 9.1: Gordon Ramsay Storefront image in Seoul, South Korea (photo taken by Henry Jenkins)

The identity of these chefs became controversial when critics called out the lack of racial and ethnic diversity and the exoticization of the performers on the *Bon Appétit* YouTube channel, part of an industry-wide push for greater diversity and inclusion. The controversy resulted in the resignation of all the existing chefs on the channel and a recasting designed to bring new personalities forward.

This shift to the celebrity chef suggests how brand sectors may build up a fan base by focusing more on the personalities of key industry figures. Something similar has developed through social media and video sharing, which has developed influencers in the make-up space or the way that Project Runway has developed and showcased the personas of next-generation fashion designers.

Steampunk

Arguably an extension of Maker Culture and thus another kind of participatory culture, the Steampunk community might be described as a fandom without an object. In this space, people come together around the fantasy that the Victorians might have successfully produced a digital culture almost a hundred years before the rise of networked computers. Certainly, there were texts that helped inspire steampunk participants—for example, Walt Disney's version of *20,000 Leagues Under the Sea* or William Gibson and Bruce Sterling's science fiction novel *The Difference Engine*. But the subculture started with people making things—technologies, mostly, but also costumes and even music—which gave these fantasies material form. Only later did commercial producers enter the picture, generating media, literature, and products targeting an existing steampunk community.

One of the key ways that targeting transpired was through references to steampunk's recognizable aesthetics, which Christine Ferguson (2011) goes so far as to call an "ideology of style." Steampunk aesthetics blend Victorian-era fashion and industrial design with futuristic technology, creating a unique retro-futuristic visual style characterized by gears, brass, leather, and steam-powered machinery (Onion, 2008). Similarly, one can be a fan of Midcentury Modern, which celebrates clean lines, organic forms, and functional elegance from the 1940s-1960s. Cottagecore, with its romanticized, rustic, and pastoral aesthetics, has also gained a dedicated following. These aesthetics, like Steampunk, inspire passionate fandoms rooted in lifestyle, design, and cultural expression.

From the start, steampunks attached themselves to the larger community of science fiction fans, which have long supported and attracted activities from NASA boosters and the above-mentioned UFO investigators to tabletop fantasy role-playing games, which were participatory but not necessarily motivated by fan passions per se. Here, the question may not be: is steampunk a fandom—by now, it clearly is—but at what point in its evolution does it make sense to call it a fandom? The answer to this question may depend on how precisely we define our terms and how well we can track the history of this community.

Amateur Adult Entertainment:

Our next fandom might be our most controversial, or at least most provocative—the amateur adult entertainment content creator community, which we read here as a type of participatory culture that attracts its own fandom. There is the mainstream adult entertainment production business, which is still largely centered on activities in the San Fernando Valley. As well as this, and increasingly intersecting with it, there is a large grassroots group of aficionados, enthusiasts, exhibitionists, and voyeurs who have long been involved in creating, sharing, and supporting each other's efforts to create and share adult entertainment outside of the formal industry. With sites like *OnlyFans*, these grassroots efforts have partially turned into platform-based content distribution, but the grassroots or "bottom-up" (perhaps gifted?) nature of some, but certainly not all, "amateur" porn production remains an important part of the culture.

We can consider the example of *Literotica*, a website for publishing and archiving erotic stories written by non-professionals that serve the desires and interests of their own community, where the roles of reader and writer are fused. This archive has much in common with the adult stories shared on a fiction site, *Archive of Our Own*, a site that is discussed throughout this series. The Archive of Our Own is a repository of a wide array of fan works, only some of which are explicit and erotic. Much like erotic fan fiction, *Literotica*'s stories extend beyond the sex act itself, grounding sex in the emotional life and interpersonal relations of their characters, considering what the sex "means," even as they also help to construct a sex-positive environment where participants can get off on shared fantasies. These stories, unlike *OnlyFans* videos, are not produced for profit; no money is exchanged amongst those reading and writing them.

We view fandom as the realm of the committed amateur or semi-professional, so part of what sets *OnlyFans* apart from fandom is how much money many people make from their work, even if they do not see themselves as part of the adult entertainment industry. There is a commercial apparatus attached to these stories, though, that supports the platform and charges for other forms of erotic expression, including audiobooks, photographs, videos, and live feeds.

Interestingly, *Literotica* has a specific forum dedicated to fan fiction and celebrity focused stories, suggesting that they see overlaps between their goals, but at the same time, these defined areas suggest that participants do not see fandom as an adequate description of their activity as a whole. We think that the site itself might better be described as a form of participatory culture. However, a look at the comments on any major entertainment site, such as Pornhub, will attest there are clearly fandoms gathering around these offerings. The fans of adult entertainers and their entertainment, whether produced in amateur or professional contexts, will celebrate, support, critique, reimagine, and derive pleasure from these creations.

The examples of UFO enthusiasts, Steampunks, and amateur adult content creators illustrate the broadness of the fandom concept and how the nature of participatory culture permeates contemporary society. They demonstrate complex and integrated forms of contemporary community and creative expression that are inter-related with media and consumer culture. They are groups that show how individuals with shared interests transcend mere audiencing or consumption to actively contribute, innovate, and influence within their spheres. This dynamic interaction greatly enriches their experi-ences with the focal object of consumption or object of fandom. It also exhibits the same fan-related challenge to the traditional bound-aries between consumer and creator, leading us to recognize them as places where people, individually and collectively, can passionately engage in vibrant cultures that are both interconnected and diverse. Although these examples stretch existing definitions of fandom, through them we may better appreciate the breadth and impact of participatory culture in contemporary society.

Do Strong Men Have Fans?

A recurring theme across the **Frames of Fandom** series will be how the contemporary media environment works by blurring once distinct categories – the fan and the consumer, the amateur and the professional, the fan and the citizen, the local and the transcultural, and many more. Our boundary cases above fit within some aspects of our definition of fandom but not others. Here, we want to consider another such example—how the global rise of autocratic and charismatic leaders and their deployment of media strategies once associated with celebrities may produce new models of citizenship that share some aspects of fandom.

Swapnil Rai is an important scholar of celebrity culture and fandom within the global south. Her book, *Networked Bollywood* (Rai, 2023), explores how powerful stars (from Raj Kapoor to Shah Ruhka Khan) reshaped the media industries centered in Mumbai into a global pop culture force to be reckoned with through their deft use of an ever-expanding range of media platforms that allow them to reach beyond national borders (initially in response to the Indian diaspora but now in pursuit of a broader range of audiences and fan communities). Rai began to notice that India's leader, Narendra Modi, was using similar tactics to reach voters in his country and to expand India's—and his own—"soft power" around the world.

Rai (2019) traces the construction of Modi as a figure who embodies religious and political traditions through his appeal to Hindu nationalism, whose appearances on reality television often construct a hypermasculine and muscular image, who is often using things like holograms to carry his message and build intimate relations with those in his country's remotest villages, and who deploys social media to give the illusion of intimate connection but to allow wider circulation of his messages. Sangita Shresthova (2020) describes efforts by Modi to lend his support and mobilized Indian-American support behind Trump in 2016 through the use of Bollywood song and dance at a Hindus for Trump rally—a form of fascist spectacle that she sees as very different from the ways Bollywood song and dance are deployed as a means of participation and voice elsewhere.

And as she talked to other scholars, Rai found that Modi was far from unique:

> A key factor that informs populist mobilization is the charismatic political leader who represents more than

their political party and has the ability to exceed political associations. Contemporary global politics is full of such leaders: Narendra Modi in India, Jair Bolsonaro in Brazil, Recep Tayyip Erdoğan in Türkiye, Rodrigo Duterte in the Philippines, Joko Widodo in Indonesia, Viktor Orbán in Hungary, Boris Johnson in the United Kingdom, and last but not the least, Donald Trump in the United States. Through figures such as these, authoritarian populist discourses are gaining prominence in the political landscape... .While there have been populist authoritarian leaders in the past, what is distinctive about twenty-first-century authoritarian populism is its celebritization. We are now in a new era in the celebritization of politics wherein strongmen leaders assume populist power through the cultivation of a celebrity-like aura within broad mediascapes. These leaders deploy the tools and tactics of celebrity that allow them to extend their public reach and connect with their followers. (Rai and Monk-Payton, 2024, 145-146)

Their populism involves not only new forms of political power and rhetorical address, but also new interfaces with their publics that tap the affordances of new media that reach voters in their everyday lives, and that addresses them through popular vernaculars. We will explore many of these same processes as they relate to more bottom-up forms of political voice and participation in **Fandom as Public** and **Fandom as Activism**. If strong men leaders are seeking to soften their autocratic images or to construct their masculine personas by becoming celebrities, they are doing so at a moment where celebrities are seeking to form intimate and affective relationships with their fans through "relational labor" (Baym, 2018).

Sebnam Baran (2024), a scholar of popular culture and fandom in Turkey and part of the circle who discussed these issues in a forum Rai helped to organize, pushes the analysis further: "Our conversations about the celebritization of politics need to include those who do the *celebrating* (i.e., fans who help turn individuals into celebrities) along with those who are celebrated." In this new political context, citizens, supporters, and followers of these powerful leaders are being reconfigured as something akin to fans. This phrase, "something akin to fans," is key here since we do not yet know how to characterize them.

Does what Susan Sontag (1975) called "fascinating fascism" produce fans? What are the implications of this analysis for fandom studies given the field's history of studying fans from a bottom-up perspective and insisting on the resistant power that fans bring with them in their encounters with celebrities and popular media, There is a risk that the analysis of the celebritization process will fall back into old models of propaganda which see messages and, in this case, affective attachments flowing down from above through various forms of manipulation and mass persuasion.

But what happens if we approach this phenomenon in a bottom-up fashion? What if we take seriously the needs being expressed, the desires being performed, and the meanings being constructed by the public even under the rule of these strongmen leaders? This is where fandom studies might make a real contribution to our understanding of international political trends. Here, Baran's short essay, which deals with the conflicts played out in Turkish social media between Turkish President Recep Tayyip Erdoğan and Turkish singer-songwriter Sezen Aksu, their respective fans and anti-fans, can only take us so far, so this remains an intriguing lacuna for other researchers to pursue more deeply.

Consider, for example, the overview we provide of debates around fan nationalism in **Fandom as Public.** Here we see a particular group of Chinese fans, known as Big Pink, war with fans from Taiwan, Korea, and other countries on fan forums. Chinese fan scholars are debating whether their nationalism is necessarily aligned with the Chinese state or whether they are redefining nationalism on their own terms through bottom-up processes paralleling how fans always redefine their fan objects to better serve their needs and desires.

To date, the majority of work in fandom studies – published in English (a key caveat) –focuses on fandom in North America, Europe, and Eastern Asia, but this is changing with an emerging generation of researchers from across the global south increasingly entering the conversation, We will be tapping their work throughout the series as it sheds light on the concepts we are discussing. Still, long term, it will also be placing new questions on the agenda and pushing us to test and refine old assumptions about what fandom is and how it works. We welcome such active revision. If fandom is a form of consumption, as we suggest above, how does it operate outside the mechanisms of the market, outside of capitalism? How does it operate under communism or under theocracy? We consider, for example, what the Disney Princesses mean in the Arab world in **Fandom as an Agent of Globalization**, finding their research suggesting that those who live in aristocratic countries perceive the role and responsibilities of being a princess – their obligations to their people – as more powerful than more personal desires to find true love, themes that capture the imagination of young western fans.

CHAPTER 10:

Frames of Fandom

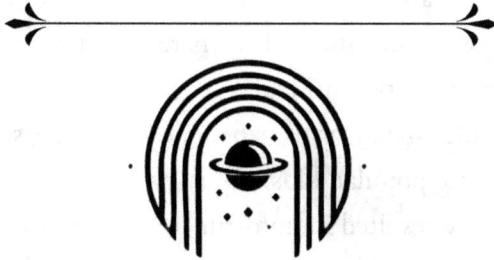

About the Book Series

Frames of Fandom is a book series intended to advance our most forward-thinking vision of what fans, scholars, and industry insiders need to know about fans and fandom. With numerous examples that cut across the gamut of fanships and fandoms, each book offers a different frame through which to examine the contemporary phenomenon of fandom. The books reflect some of our experiences and discoveries as Fandom Studies and consumer culture researchers. The juxtaposition of these two fields may sometimes be jarring since fandom studies start with a much greater skepticism and even resistance to business interests than consumer culture research does. The industry gets much wrong about fans, often acting in ways that damage, trivialize, and exploit their culture. We consider many of these critiques. But we also understand that fans operate in the West within consumer capitalism and will inevitably be drawn into close relationships with commercial franchises and brands. The question is what kinds of relationships they will have, and that is the central question that drives this series.

Beyond combining fandom studies with brand research, other elements of our approach are also unique. First, these are books about *fandoms*, not fans. Their perspective shifts from thinking about isolated individual audience perceptions to embracing the collective dimension of fandoms, which is increasingly interrelated with technologies and devices. Second, this series of books explores the fan universe around the globe. There have been historic divides in fandom studies between media, sports, and music fandoms that mirror the divides many of us experienced in high school between nerds, jocks, and popular kids. As it has within academic fields, these divides have resulted in unfortunate silos. Sports fandoms were largely studied as part of sports science faculties and journals, while music studies handled music fandoms. Cultural and media studies focused, for the most part, on literary and media fandoms and only occasionally touched upon sports and music fandoms. Consumer researchers dabbled here and there, but mainly framed fandoms as related to brand gatherings. We are trying, the best our own expertise allows, to cut across those divisions here to show what these various kinds of fandoms, brandoms, brand communities, and subcultures of consumption have in common. Furthermore, we make major efforts to include, as best as we can, the full range of race, gender, ethnic, sexual orientation, and other social positions, and also to include representation from around the world and not just the more intensely studied American and European fandom contexts.

So, whether you are a student delving into the particulars of modern fan cultures, a brand manager seeking to unlock the potential of fan engagement, or a fan activist wondering how fandom might offer resources for social change movements, we have designed this series to offer you something that we hope will be valuable and unique.

Defining Fandom: Book 1

Defining Fandom is the first book in the Frames of Fandom series. Here, we define and discuss the nature of fans, fanship, and fandom. **Defining Fandom** provides a fundamental conceptual grounding in the notion of fans, fanships, and fandoms; we introduce the auto-ethnographic style of the series, which draws heavily from the aca-fan tradition and the work both authors have written in that modality. Here, we define fans as people who passionately engage with their "fan object," which is not a physical object but a media or consumer culture production like EXO, James Bond, or Boca Juniors (or, in Rob and Henry's cases, Batman, Famous Monsters, Doctor Who, Star Trek, Led Zeppelin, Patti Smith, Dune, The Beatles, and many others).

As fan activity becomes more social, involving people such as friends and family, it stretches into fanship. Fans become members of a fandom when they join a collective of others who share their passion and interest in the fan object and partake in participatory culture. Being a fan and partaking in fanship are personal states or identities; being in fandom is connection and affiliation. Fandoms are composed of some of the most passionate, connected, creative, critical, and/or active fans. Fandoms gives participants an outlet through which they celebrate, support, critique, reimagine, and derive pleasure from the activities related to the object of their fandom. We use the definitions from **Defining Fandom** as the foundation on which we build and expand across the series.

Fandom as Audience: Book 2

Building on the basis established in **Defining Fandom**, our next book examines the established communication and sociological perspective that seeks to understand fandoms by conceptualizing them as a type of audience. Understanding this perspective requires background on the way scholars, as well as marketers, have approached audiences. The book takes readers on a deep dive into the intellectual history of audience research and audience studies that bridges from the Birmingham School's initial development of the cultural studies field starting in the late 1950s and the origins of fandom studies in the early 1990s highlighting fandoms as complex emergent phenomena that encompass media consumption, cultural debate, and creative expression. Many key works in audience research centered on texts which attracted significant fan interests and also spoke to the global circulation and reception of fan objects. Eventually, the view of the passive audience gives way to a much more informed and active, even adoring, audience. This book seeks to convey a rich understanding of their underpinnings, origins, and key principles by including views of fandom as an audience, the role of representation and fantasy, and the core tension between fascination and frustration that drives fandom related activities. The book also analyzes and critiques concepts of market segmentation and its intimate relationship with audience research as it seeks to develop practical applications of this viewpoint. The book closes with a discussion of fandom as an interpretive community and how one learns to read as a fan. **Fandom as Audience** provides readers with a grounded and realistic approach to audience and fandom studies, as well as new ways to think about segmentation and marketing research on different types of "audiences."

Fandom as Consumer Collective: Book 3

The interrelationship of consumer culture with fandom colors our framing of the third book of our series, **Fandom as Consumer Collective.** After exploring the definition of consumers and consumer culture, this book challenges traditional views of consumers as isolated rational decision-makers and conveys the significant body of consumer culture research examining consumers as collective and passionately engaged. Contemporary consumer culture studies provide a complex and variable framework for understanding how fans collectively engage with and shape their environments through market-based resources. The c hapter d evelops t he c oncept o f e lective a ffinities—social connections based on shared values and interests—and looks at how fandoms demonstrate the active, communal, and dynamic nature of consumption that permeates important marketing concepts such as subcultures of consumption, virtual communities of consumption, and brand communities. The role of collective storytelling as well as shared values, rituals and language shape these collective consumer identities and behaviors. Viewed through this lens, consumer collectives and fandoms begin to blur into one another. The result is a call for a much more situated and nuanced understanding of fandoms and consumer culture as connected realms that are constantly being co-constructed by various individuals, groups, businesses, and technologies. Book 3 offers a reconceptualization of both fandom and the consumer collective concept that highlights the transformative power of collective consumer engagements in shaping today's global business and cultural landscapes.

Fandom as Subculture: Book 4

One of the most pervasive and powerful conceptual frames applied to fandom studies has been that of subcultures because, when fandom studies emerged as a distinctive field of inquiry, it built directly on earlier bodies of research on media audiences and on subcultures that emphasize identity development and opposition to mainstream norms. This research and its background form a substantial literature that this book overviews, explains, and synthesizes for the contemporary reader. To illustrate what fandom studies took from earlier research on subcultures, **Fandom as Subculture** explores a phenomenon known as Disneybounding. Disney Bounding reflects an attempt to work around policies at the Disney Theme

Parks intended to restrict adult "guests" from dressing up like their favorite characters, which might cause confusion between fans and park employees. To evade these policies, these fans abstracted out from the specific character designs to tap colors and patterns associated with those figures. A community has grown up around these everyday forms of cosplay, whether performed in the parks, in one's own neighborhoods, or online.

As the book explains, Disney Bounding displays many of the traits often associated with subcultural fashion: discrimination amongst potential fan objects; affiliation with a larger social community with shared interests; the construction of new identities; the acquisition of shared meanings and the mastery over distinctive bodies of knowledge; passion and affect; new forms of expression and interpretation; appropriation and resignification of elements from the dominant culture. Much as "cool hunters" have learned to study subcultural style as a source for innovation whether in the design of fashion, the development of products, or the deployment of new forms of marketing, media producers and marketers are increasingly studying fandom to develop new insights into the development and promotion of media content. Subcultures fascinate sociologists, media scholars, and marketers alike because of their local practices, languages, styles, and ideologies. Members of established subcultures may also serve as opinion leaders for much wider audiences or markets that are not part of the core subculture, and they may even be copied and marketed for mainstream consumption. Certain established subcultures, such as e-girls, WitchTok, or dark academia, appear to have a broad appeal that transcends national and cultural boundaries, demographic cohorts, as well as racial, ethnic, and class disparities in reach and influence. For all these reasons, studying fandom through a subcultural frame is a rich and productive pursuit.

Fandom as Co-Creation: Book 5

Creativity is king in the content economy, and a long literature in both marketing and fandom studies reveals the value of fandoms and consumer collectives in furthering acts of original production. There is a complex interrelationship between creativity, innovation, and fandom within cultural and business contexts that this book seeks to thoroughly uncover. **Fandom as Co-creation** explores the foundational principle that creativity is a driver of both cultural evolution and business innovation. **Fandom as Co-creation** transitions traditional concepts of lone genius investors into the concept of "co-creation," a collaborative process involving businesses and consumers working together to generate value. These various acts of value creation are not limited to economic benefits, although they are certainly important to business. They also extend to the creation of cultural and social enrichment, especially within fandoms. **Fandom as Co-creation** challenges the traditional business-centric view of innovation, highlighting the creative contributions of fans in redefining and expanding brand and cultural landscapes. Certainly, framing **Fandom as Co-creation** means that various fan activities can be seen as forms of labor, work, or even capital that contribute significantly to the cultural and business sectors–and also can be exploited or rewarded. Book 5 discusses numerous fandom-driven innovations influencing larger market trends and business strategies. The book also emphasizes the potential to leverage the creative potential of fandoms in co-creation processes by encouraging an inclusive approach that values the contributions of fandom's astoundingly creative members.

Fandom as Participatory Culture: Book 6

With the fifth book detailing fandom's creative innovations, the sixth book discusses what – and how – fans create for themselves, centering our discussion around the core concept of participatory culture. The book considers how participatory culture mediates between two more widely understood categories, that of folk culture and mass culture, arguing that participatory culture applies a folk culture logic to materials drawn from mass culture. We identify some of the mechanisms that encourage participation in cultural practices defined by relatively low thresholds of entry. Running throughout **Fandom as Participatory Culture** is a consideration of fandom as what sociologist Howard Becker (1982/2008) called an "art world," a social formation with its own aesthetic goals and norms, its own institutions of production, circulation, and critique. Fan fiction is often ridiculed as bad writing and some of it is bad by any definition. Fan fiction communities have a greater tolerance for immature or incompetent writing, allowing them to provide a place where new talent can be recruited, make mistakes, get feedback, and grow better over time. We will also discuss how new models of participatory learning in the field of learning science have emerged by closely studying how the fan art world operates. The growing visibility of participatory culture in a networked culture has been a transformative force in the 21st century, but most of us most of the time are still consuming culture produced by the creative industries. We are still, in many ways, an audience. **Fandom as Participatory Culture** concludes by considering the limits of participatory culture, starting with the recognition that while we may inhabit a <u>more</u> participatory culture, not every person is allowed or able to participate due to various kinds on limitations on inclusion, of access to technology, to knowledge and other resources, to mentorship, and so forth.

Fandom as Public: Book 7

Fandom as Public reflects some of the insights that have emerged from understanding fandom as a public sphere, as a place where public opinion is formed and mobilized. In Book 7, we return to our earlier focus on fandoms as media audiences to lay out some of the important distinctions between audiences and publics. In a nutshell, audiences pay attention while publics demand attention. Fandom as a public can rally people together around shared concerns and can exert pressure on the media industries themselves, holding them accountable for decisions they make, which might have what fans perceive as negative effects on the culture. We might consider what historian Michael Saler has described as "public spheres of the imagination" where real-world issues are discussed through the lens of fictional worlds. Book 7 discusses how the letter columns of comic books mirror those of earlier publications as sites of debate and conversation. It also discusses what fandom studies might have to teach us about unruly and toxic publics such as Q-Anon which contributed to the January 6 insurrection in 2021 and also the ways that the ASMR community provided a therapeutic public during the COVID pandemic, where informal community leaders encouraged the self-care and mental health support lacking elsewhere in the culture.

Conceptualizing fandom not just as groups of fans but as active publics and important stakeholders draws attention to the shifting power relations of modern media. Throughout **Fandom as Public**, we juxtapose what fandom studies have taught us about fan publics with the models of publics that have helped to inform the evolving practices of the public relations (PR) field. A promising recent development considers public relations as a way to understand how to get diverse publics to communicate effectively and relate collaboratively with one another. Embracing this undertaking, the **Fandom as Public** emphasizes the full power of fandoms to shape social spaces and public discourse in the digital age. Overall, **Fandom as Public** begins to chart a new set of practices, which we develop fully in **Fandom Relations**, that encompass a more ethical, respectful, and mutually beneficial approach to public and marketplace engagement with fandoms.

Fandom as Activism: Book 8

Fandom as Activism picks up where **Fandom as Public** leaves off, taking us deeper into the relationship between fandom and other movements for social change. Book 8 expands our frame on fandom further, moving from a consideration of theories of the public sphere to sociologically informed accounts of social movements. In writing about Madonna and her fans, John Fiske discussed the ways that her music and persona encouraged young women, in particular, to question the constraints on their lives, to claim more of a presence for themselves in public, to create a different relationship with their bodies, to form communities with other fans, and ultimately, to promote forms of popular feminism as they relate to what he described as the "micropolitics" of everyday life. Continuing our recurring references to Star Trek, we discuss the famed letter-writing campaign that sought to get the series renewed when it was under threat of cancellation and the ways it has provided a model for subsequent Save Our Show campaigns. We also return to a key question in early fan research on why or why not fans regard themselves as feminists, suggesting that early Star Trek fandom might be understood as responding to the emergence of sex-positive feminism around the same moment in time. The book further illustrates how fandom activities, like the Harry Potter Alliance (now Fandom Forward), transform fan engagement into political activism, rallying around causes such as literacy and equality. Book 8 underscores how the members of fandoms leverage their collective power to effect substantial change by shaping public discourse and influencing broader shifts in culture and society. Using China as an example, we also consider the growing phenomenon of fan nationalism and the ways it does or does not connect with the needs of the State. **Fandom as Activism**'s explorations highlight the powerful mix of passion and politics present in fandom. It takes the discussion further by arguing how this knowledge can serve as a blueprint for contemporary fans and organizers aiming to harness the transformative power of fan communities.

Fandom as Desire: Book 9

Passion has played a central role in this book series, from the definition of fans as the passionately engaged to the passion of innovative co-creators, resistant subculture members, and mobilized activists. In **Fandom as Desire**, we delve into the emotional, psychological, and socio-economic forces that drive fandoms, viewing them as central to understanding and collaboration. Opening with an extended fandom-related shopping sequence by one of the authors, the book seeks to derive a range of novel theoretical perspectives on fandom from deep personal insight. Framing fandom as a complex collective site of manifold consumer desires prompts us to decipher the role of materiality and embodiment within fandom. We find fans' connections to objects such as collectible merchandise often playing a powerful role in their fan identities and community connections and, conscious of prior critiques, we embrace this materiality in a way few other books on fandom previously have. We leverage the energetic desire theories of Deleuze and Guattari to present fandom as a network of desires, a system in which fans are constantly in flux, seeking out different types of connection, innovating, and collectively and collaboratively working with their bodies' energies. Related to this theory, and setting the stage for the **Fandom as Techoculture** and **Fandom and Technocapitalism** books to come, we explore the role of digital platforms in shaping the desires that mold fandom. Algorithms and affordances, it turns out, play key roles in connecting fans with the objects of their fandom and with each other. In addition, seeing **Fandom as Desire** offers us a springboard to discuss desires for a better world. Book 9's final sections examine in some depth the important utopian longings that have long linked people to fandoms by acknowledging their underlying and often under-acknowledged potential for social commentary and change. Here, we identify ways that fandom studies has been responding to the affective turn in the humanities, considering how writers such as Sarah Ahmed and Ann Cvetkovich might reframe our object of study.

Fandom as Devotion: Book 10

Numerous prior scholars have examined the relationship between fandom and religious beliefs and behaviors in ways ranging from thorough to facile. Book 10 seeks to take on the complex and controversy-laden relationship between fandom activities and devotional practices in the subtle and nuanced manner that the topic deserves. As Book 9 did, **Fandom as Devotion** opens with a personal recounting about one of the authors' ritualistic teen musical outings. This personal perspective set the stage for the most auto-ethnographic book since **Defining Fandom**. Like Book 1, auto-ethnography is used to introduce and then explore conceptual topics. Here, our different backgrounds and experiences lead us to different conceptual paths in our exploration of how fandom can manifest as a form of devotion. **Fandom as Devotion** likens some aspects of fandom to traditional religious practices, such as the veneration of music icons like Taylor Swift or Harry Styles. It complicates these simple analogies, however. Lacking a formal governance structure, fandom may be situated within a liminal space that is both powerful and unofficial. Fandom often co-exists with other religious beliefs and practices, being drawn into their orbit as the fan object may evoke forms of spirituality rather than competing with religion. Ultimately, **Fandom as Devotion** presents a careful argument about the role of fandom as a source of meaningful and significant life experiences. It suggests that fandom provides a space for personal and communal expression, often fulfilling emotional and spiritual needs in ways that parallel traditional religious communities.

Fandom as Agent of Globalization: Book 11

To apply the frame of **Fandom as Agent of Globalization**, we first must tackle the relatively simple critiques of cultural imperialism which so often surface when we discuss the global circulation of popular culture: the idea that American media producers dominate the world markets and in doing so, spread core ideological assumptions underlying western capitalism. In fact, a growing number of countries are producing film and television content that circulates beyond their borders, often in unanticipated ways. Streaming services such as Netflix play a vital role in this process. To operate in different markets, they also must coproduce local content, which they in turn circulate to other markets, increasing access to content from diverse countries. Book 11 calls this "the global shuffle," and it changes what media gets consumed by Americans as much or more than it changes the flow of American content into Asia, Latin America, Africa, or Europe. In some ways, the global shuffle was anticipated by fan culture's early embrace of Hong Kong action films, Japanese anime, Bollywood genre films, Bollywood and Hallyu. Fans play active grassroots roles in preparing markets for these international imports, helping to identify content that might play well to local audiences, sometimes preparing the way with amateur fan-subbed versions, and educating the public about how to read unfamiliar genres. A powerful and dynamic cultural exchange, the global shuffle represents the world's shift from a unidirectional flow of media to a much more multilateral dialogue. Like the changes in global fandoms themselves, this transformation reshapes how narratives are consumed and appreciated worldwide. Fandom, in this context, becomes a powerful conduit for cultural understanding and exchange. Fandom educates, enables and empowers diverse audiences to engage with and influence the global media landscape.

Locations of Fandom: Book 12

This book builds on the globalizing insights from Book 11, seeking to better understand the idea of transnational and transcultural fandoms through investigating the local sites where fandom is performed and pop cultural capital gets appraised. Here, we respond to a call from several recent scholars to adopt a "pedestrian" or ground-level perspective on fandom's material practices and how they operate in particular cultural landscapes. **Locations of Fandom** draws heavily – but not exclusively – on examples from East Asian countries, especially Japan, Korea, and China. These fan locations operate on diverse scales – from individual malls or retail chains to local neighborhoods to cities to nations – and different temporalities – from pop-up fan events or recurring conventions, such as San Diego Comic-Con, to longstanding commercial establishments such as Disneyland. The locations are where this book discovers local and global media industries interacting with subcultural entrepreneurs and creators to shape how these works are received by a larger public. Drawing insights from cultural geography and tourism research, Book 12 will consider different sites of fan production and consumption, different forms of fan engagement, different fan practices, and different material cultures that grow up around specific fan communities.

Fandom as Technoculture: Book 13

The Internet and subsequent Web 2.0, social media, platformization, and app revolutions have forever altered the face of fandom. However, fandom has had a long history of early engagement with and innovative uses of technology, stretching back at least to the mid-1800s when rail travel allowed Franz Liszt's live performances to conquer a large swath of Europe. **Fandom as Technoculture** provides readers with a detailed exploration of how media consumption has transformed from a casual leisure activity into a technologically mediated behavior with significant social, psychological, economic, and, especially, cultural implications. **Fandom as Technoculture** explores this theme by examining a range of fan phenomena, including binge-watching, the affordances of podcasting and new technologies such as generative visual AI but also fan practices around amateur printing presses, early radio, the production and distribution of zines, and so forth. With a strong historical emphasis that uses numerous examples to explore how technology and fandom have co-evolved, Book 13 in the series is focused squarely on some of the tensions between agency and structure inherent in technology usage.

Fandom and Technocapitalism: Book 14

The interrelationships of technology and capitalism had major effects on almost every element of society, including fandom, and this book examines those effects. Building on and extending Book 13's critical elements, **Fandom and Technocapitalism** examines a range of platforms, phenomena, practices, and structures to inform a novel understanding of the ways in which digital capitalism shape fandoms, and vice versa. It employs several theoretical positions to achieve this, including networks of desire, affordance theory, practice theory, technology enchantment, and technology as ideology. **Fandom and Technocapitalism** takes a penetrating and critical look at how fan culture intertwines with contemporary capitalism, affecting both fandom and businesses and how these developments have been studied across the social sciences. The book lays out technocapitalism as a powerful economic system where devices and technologies are used by media, entertainment, and technology industries to monetize fan passion and engagement. The digital ecosystem quantifies fannish engagement, leveraging this information across various platforms for economic gain, and fans respond to these moves; these intertwined social, technological, and economic processes have important cultural, social, and psychological ramifications. The chapter discusses how fan creativity and content become contested terrains, both violations of property rights and valuable corporate assets. It addresses the legal and digital strategies that manipulate fan interactions, turning organic fan culture into a structured asset that businesses can exploit. **Fandom and Technocapitalism** focuses its critiques on the ongoing shift from organic fan engagement to monetizable interactions, providing insights into the broader impacts for fans, society, and the evolving digital economy. By exploring these central themes, we hope to provide a comprehensive understanding of the dynamic space of fandom in the digital age and the entangled give-and-take between technology, culture, and human agency–and the powerful economic force of capitalism that currently define them.

Fandom Relations: Book 15

The final book of our series, **Fandom Relations**, is also the most speculative. It seeks to reconceptualize fandom not just as a form of leisure or entertainment based collective but as a significant, pervasive social structure influencing global politics, media, culture, and society. Throughout the **Frames of Fandom** series we will be building this perspective, with each book contributing nuanced explorations into the varied facets of fandom—ranging from its role as a public and subculture, to consumer collective, co-creative group, agent of globalization, and site of activism and technocapitalist resistance.

The foundational premise of **Fandom Relations** lies in an ethical recalibration of the ways organization and institutions view and engage with fandoms. Recognizing fandoms as crucial cultural resources, a crucible of sorts, may impel us to consider what a society would look like where we took fandom seriously as a social form. **Fandom Relations** considers such a society, envisioning it as one where local and global citizens will be encouraged to unite and form collectives and can be engaged passionately as active co-creators, cultural critics, and community builders. Illuminating fandom through categories such as devotion, desire, and participatory culture, the closing book in the **Frames of Fandom** series asserts that the acts of fandoms include transformative engagements that reframe identities, community ties, and cultural narratives. These activities position fans to question mainstream norms and to use collective forms as vehicles for personal and collective empowerment. Moreover, these acts teach citizen-consumers a form of public activism, shape market-defining consumer practices, and hold the potential to foster global connections that transcend geographical, political, and cultural barriers. We use this book to question and reframe the notion of the commodification of fan labor while celebrating the communitarian and activist spirit fandoms often bring. We have been clear-eyed and practical for the first fourteen books, but the vision of **Fandom Relations** is ultimately upbeat and utopian. We seek to leverage fandoms and their study to broaden the scope of how we understand markets, cultures, and institutions, positioning fandom as a passionate and potent element of contemporary life that offers new paths to understand and pursue identity, community, and resistance.

What Comes Next?

As a series, **Frames of Fandom** has a mission not only to inform pedagogy and postulation but also to influence practice and policy. Our aspiration is to formulate a clear statement of the ways this might take place in **Fandom Relations**, our fifteenth and final book in the series. Fandom Relations is also the name of the course we co-teach at USC Annenberg, and with this name we pay homage to the students and the many others who helped bring these ideas to fruition. Throughout the book series, our approach is founded on the recognition of the social value of fans and fandoms and their contributions as significant participants in the media ecosystem, in culture, and in society.

We welcome your ideas and your feedback on how to do this better. As our overview of **Fandom as Public** disclosed, the field of public relations has been shifting to understanding how to facilitate greater communication and collaboration between various publics. This shift is fundamental and important; we find ourselves intrigued by its possibilities and position our ideas of a Fandom Relations field within it. This, and the vital notion of relationships, including brand relationships, that informs this book, are why we have decided to call this new orientation Fandom *Relations*.

In many of the books in the **Frames of Fandom** series, we will be closing with our attempt to overview some of the key implications of the book for a greater understanding and appreciation of fans and fandom. In this book, which serves as an introduction to the interface between consumer culture research and fandom studies, we believe that this broadening of perspective creates a "big tent" effect, which should draw managerial attention to the many productive overlaps and intersections of fans and consumers.

We hope that you have enjoyed the big tent approach of **Frames of Fandom** and invite you to continue thinking, discussing, and wondering about the captivating world of fandom.

GLOSSARY

Acafan: An academic who is also a fan of the media they study, blending their professional insights with personal passion to enrich both their scholarly work, research analysis, and fan engagements.

Adult Fan: An adult who passionately engages with media or entertainment content that is typically marketed towards children or adolescents, such as Disney films, the *My Little Pony* series, or LEGO. The term underscores the significance of these cultural interactions in the lives of adults, highlighting their creative, social, and emotional investments in content often perceived as intended for a younger audience. Adult fans demonstrate the permeability of age boundaries in media consumption, showcasing how fandom transcends generational divides and contributes to a broad sense of identity and community.

Affirmational Fandom: A mode of fan engagement which is often aspirational in its hopes of learning how the fan object was produced, identifying with the creators/authors and hoping to learn things which might allow the fan to enter the creative industries. Its core value is mastery of the lore and production history of the fan object, values often associated with fan masculinities.

Affordances: The possibilities for action or goal fulfillment provided by a particular object or environment. In the context of digital media, affordances refer to the properties of a technology that enable specific actions for users. For fandom, these are the features of digital platforms that allow fans to engage, create, and share content.

Brand Management: The application of marketing techniques to a specific product, product line, or brand to increase its value over time. It involves managing the tangible and intangible characteristics of the brand to ensure that it remains appealing to consumers.

Bronies: Adult fans of My Little Pony, often gay men. Because they are so different from the assumed audience, they are often depicted by the news media and even some academics as perverse.

Civic Imagination: The capacity to envision alternative futures through the lens of fandom (but really any story including folk, religious, or personal) which allows us to envision ourselves as civic agents capable of making change, to model an alternative to current practices, to map a process for making change, to develop a shared sense of collective action, to forge bonds with others whose perspectives differ from our own, to taste freedom before we have directly experienced it, and to charge everyday spaces with civic meaning. Stories, including those from popular culture, become resources we use to imagine otherwise.

Co-Creation: The collaborative process between fans and producers or brands to create new content or products. This interaction emphasizes the creative input of fans and can lead to innovative developments in media and products.

Consumer: An individual who engages with and utilizes various cultural and media products and services from within a market-mediated social environment. This engagement is not passive; rather, consumers actively choose, interpret, shape, and sometimes even redefine the products they consume through their cultural and social practices. The term highlights the role of individuals in the broader cultural and economic systems where they choose, purchase, use, and dispose of various goods and services. It also emphasizes their ongoing contributions to the collective co-creation of cultural meanings and social relationships. This active participation can extend to the co-creation of content, as seen in fan cultures where members of fandoms, who are also consumers, are deeply involved in the production of new creative works and community-driven activities based on shared interests and passions.

Consumer Collective: A concept where fans are viewed not only as consumers but also as active participants in cultural and economic systems. Fans contribute to and influence the cultural landscape through their creative and critical engagements with media and brands.

Cultural (or subcultural) Capital: The social assets (skills, styles, recognition) of an individual that promote social mobility but are not always economically based, often influential in fan communities for gaining status or influence. In the context of fandom, (sub)cultural capital refers to the knowledge, skills, and competencies that fans accumulate which enable them to gain status and influence within their communities.

Cultural Imperialism: The dominance of one culture over others, often through the dissemination of media and cultural products that impose certain values or practices.

Disney Bounding: A fan subcultural practice associated with the Disney theme parks. Because the parks restricted adult fans from dressing in costumes, the fans responded by developing costumes that build on the color palette and design elements of the Disney characters, allowing them to develop a more playful attitude and to signal subcultural identities to other participants.

Encoding and Decoding: A media theory conceptualized by Stuart Hall that suggests media messages are encoded by their creators with certain meanings and decoded by audiences who may interpret them in varying ways depending on cultural and personal contexts.

Ethical Stanning: A practice where fans support celebrities and public figures not only based on their popularity or talent but also on how well they align with ethical values and social justice issues.

Fan Activism: The actions taken by fans to use their passion for media to effect social change, often aligning with larger social movement goals.

Fan Engagement: The involvement of fans in both consuming and actively interacting with media content, often characterized by activities like content creation, community participation, and social media interaction.

Fan Economy: Economic activities generated by fandom, including the buying and selling of fan-made products, attending conventions, and participating in fan-based crowdfunding efforts.

Fanon: Fan-created elements and interpretations of a media content that do not necessarily align with the official canon but are accepted among members of the fan community.

Fan Fiction: Creative content generated by fans that uses existing characters and worlds from popular media (like movies, books, or games) to develop new stories, often shared within fan communities.

Fandom: A vibrant culture of passionate engagement through which individuals or groups celebrate, support, critique, reimagine, and derive pleasure from a specific interest or activity. Fans engage in a variety of activities related to their interests, forming communities that foster a sense of identity and collective engagement.

Fandom Relations: A proposed scientific field and ethical approach to working with fandoms founded on the recognition of the social value of fans and fandoms and their contributions as significant participants in the media ecosystem.

Fanship: A personal identity associated with individual enjoyment and appreciation of a specific band, series, or other interests, without necessarily engaging in a wider community or creative activities. This contrasts with fandom, which is a collective identity shared among fans.

Fan Studies: An academic subfield focused on understanding individual fans, their practices, identities, and relationships with the objects of their fandom.

Fandom Studies: An academic subfield related to fan studies that examines the social and collective aspects of fan activities, focusing on how fans interact with each other and form communities around shared interests.

Global Shuffle: A dynamic movement of media content across global boundaries facilitated by digital platforms, which reshapes local media landscapes by introducing diverse cultural content often without regard to traditional trade routes or geopolitical alliances..

Grassroots Circulation: The sharing and promotion of content through fan networks without the direct involvement of traditional media outlets, often enhancing the reach and impact of fan-created or favored content.

Grassroots Media: Media forms that are created, circulated, and consumed at the community level as opposed to being produced by centralized, professional media outlets; these media forms often align with local interests and perspectives.

Immersion: The sensation of being engulfed in an alternative reality, much as a swimmer may feel cut off from the world as they plunge into watery depths. Immersion may refer to properties of the performance context as in immersive theater, properties of a medium such as VR or AR which seem to engulf us inside its fictional world, properties of audience engagement and conceptual framing such as those associated with fandom or even properties of branding.

Janus Principle: a social notion proposed by Arthur Koestler wherein every fundamental element of a structural system in all healthy social systems (including bodies, communities, and systems of knowledge) exhibits dual propensities. One propensity is to seek autonomy, while the other strives for integration with larger the larger system or subsystems. Koestler's principle is metaphorically linked to Janus, the Roman god with two faces, symbolizing transitions and duality—looking inward to individual autonomy and outward towards collective integration. Applied to the context of fandom and individual fans, it captures the inherent opposition between acting as an independent individual and as an organized member of a collective. Thus, it, draws attention to the sophisticated interaction between personal identity and collective social processes within fan communities

Mass Culture: A broad generic term for culture that is mass produced, mass distributed, and mass consumed. This term emerges from critical responses to the culture industries and tends to carry negative connotations.

Media Literacy: The ability to access, analyze, evaluate, create, and act using all forms of communication. In the context of fandom, it involves a critical understanding of how media content is produced, interpreted, and its broader societal impacts. The Media Literacy movement has undergone three distinctive phases focused on critical consumption, critical production, and critical participation.

Participatory Culture: A concept describing communities and cultural practices where participants actively engage in creation and circulation around shared interests, learning from each other and organizing socially to promote common goals. Members of a participatory culture are not passive consumers or audience members, but contribute to the media and content they love, often creating new works and engaging in discussions that enrich and expand the original material.

Participatory Learning: Educational practices that leverage the principles of participatory culture to foster learning environments where students actively engage in creating, sharing, and collaborating.

Participatory Politics: Political engagement facilitated by participatory cultures, where individuals and groups use media platforms to engage in social activism and advocacy.

Popular Culture: forms of culture or cultural objects that have been embraced as a resource by fans and other consumers and integrated into their everyday life world, particularly as an aspect of their communication with others.

Prosumer: A portmanteau of producer and consumer, referring to individuals who produce content, goods, or services rather than solely consuming them. This term reflects a blurring of the distinctions between consumers and producers, particularly in digital and media contexts.

Produser: A portmanteau of producer and user, referring to participants in new web projects, such as Wikipedia or more generally Web 2.0 practices, where users generate much of the content they consume through formal and informal systems of production.

Relational Labor: The effort put into maintaining personal and emotional connections with others, particularly in professional contexts. This term is often used in discussions about the interactions between celebrities and their fans via social media.

Re-storying: Starting from the premise that the dominant stories in a culture encompass particular forms of power, the reimagining of those stories as resources for a more just and equitable society. A central element in the current narrative change movement, with fandom often cited as a core example because it illustrates the capacity to rewrite stories to better reflect the interests of their audience.

Social Economy: A framework within fandom studies that views fan activities as contributing to both cultural value and economic value, recognizing the dual role of fans as consumers and creators.

Stan: Derived from the Eminem song of the same name, a "stan" is used to describe a "superfan" who is highly devoted, often to the point of being obsessive. It originally had a somewhat negative connotation, implying excessive or unhealthy fandom, but has since evolved to be used more broadly to express enthusiastic support.

Stanning: This is the verb form of "stan" and refers to the act of being an avid fan of someone or something. It implies actively following, promoting, and supporting a particular figure or franchise with great enthusiasm and loyalty.

Subcultural Entrepreneurship: Fans or individuals who leverage their subcultural capital to create new business opportunities or cultural products that resonate with specific fan communities.

Subculture: A group within a larger culture with distinct values, norms, and interests, often manifested through distinctive styles, behaviors, and beliefs. In the context of fandom, subcultures are often formed around specific interests or media properties.

Transcultural Fandom: The phenomenon where fan practices and cultures cross national and cultural boundaries, fueled by a mix of access and affinity, contributing to a global exchange of ideas and media content.

Transformational Fandom: A mode of fan engagement which creatively and critically rewrites the source material to make it more reflective of their own desires, identities, and experiences, often discussed in contrast with affirmational fandom. This mode is often associated with women, queer people, and fans of color whose interests are often marginalized in the source material but can be brought to the surface by fan fiction and other forms of fanworks.

Transmedia Storytelling: A narrative structure that extends across multiple media platforms, allowing for a more immersive and comprehensive exploration of the story and its characters, with each medium contributing uniquely to the viewer's understanding of the story.

Tribalism: A sociocultural phenomenon where individuals strongly identify with and exhibit a sense of loyalty to specific groups or communities, often characterized by shared interests, values, or cultural traits. In fandom, members often form tight-knit groups that are deeply connected through common passions for specific media, brands, or cultural phenomena. The term also underscores the protective and sometimes exclusionary behaviors that may arise within these groups, reflecting both the solidarity and the potential for divisiveness inherent in such strong group identifications.

User-Generated Content: Media content created and submitted by consumers or fans rather than by professional media producers and advertisers. This content can include videos, blogs, discussion posts, digital images, audio files, and other forms of media.

EXERCISE

Personal Fan Narrative and Autoethnography

When we teach our fan relations class, we ask our students to start by writing autobiographical essays that describes how they became fans and what that relationship has meant in their lives. Students are prompted to write essays detailing their personal journeys into fandom, and this reflection allows them to introspect and examine how fan identities and activities have shaped their lives. These narratives are more than personal accounts; they provide an introspective chronicle of their engagement with media and cultural entities and also help us to conceptualize and broaden what we conceive of as a fandom.

This exercise is valuable because it helps illuminate the complex inner and outer linkages many of us have to our fandoms. Being a fan becomes an epistemology—a distinct way of knowing—which fandom studies, from the start and inspired by Angela McRobbie's work, came to value as a way of better understanding the fan cultures we sought to document.

The object is to explore and articulate personal fan experiences, identifying the social, cultural, and emotional aspects that contribute to the development of fan identities. This exercise aims to enhance understanding of the intricate connections between individual narratives and broader fan cultures.

Instructions:

1. Write up a Personal Narrative

   - Begin by writing a reflective essay that traces your journey into fandom. Describe the moment or series of events that led you to become a fan. This could be a particular book, show, game, event, or community that resonated with you.

   - Detail the evolution of your fandom. How has it grown or changed over time? What activities do you engage in as a fan (e.g., collecting, creating fan art, participating in forums, attending conventions)?

   - Reflect on your chosen fandom's role in your life. Consider questions such as:

   - How has being a part of this fandom shaped your identity?

   - What friendships, communities, or networks have you formed as a result of this fandom?

   - Have there been any significant life decisions influenced by your fan interests?

2. Dive into your cultural exploration

   - Examine the cultural and social aspects of your fandom. What does your fandom say about cultural trends, social issues, or the current state of media?

   - How does your fan community interact with and interpret the content differently from the mainstream audience?

   - Analyze how the media property or activity you are a fan of addresses issues such as diversity, representation, and inclusion.

3. Try Autoethnographic or Auto-netnographic Analysis

   • Using your personal narrative as a case study, conduct an autoethnographic analysis. Identify and discuss the broader cultural patterns and themes that emerge from your story.

   • Consider how your experience within a fandom intersects with your other identities (e.g., gender, ethnicity, nationality, age). How does this intersectionality impact your fan experience?

   • Discuss the ways in which being a fan has influenced your understanding of the world and your place in it. Has fandom altered your perspective on certain issues or led you to engage in advocacy or activism?

4. Imbue your work with scholarly context

   • Incorporate at least three academic sources related to fandom studies to support your analysis. These could be articles, book chapters, or theoretical frameworks that provide insight into fan culture and identity.

   • Reflect on how these scholarly perspectives align with or contrast your personal fan experience.

5. Present and Discuss

   • Prepare to present the key points of your narrative and analysis to your class or study group.

   • Engage in a discussion with your peers about the commonalities and differences in your fan experiences. What can these narratives collectively tell us about the nature of fandom and its role in society?

   • Conclude by writing a short reflection on what you learned from the exercise, both from your own introspection and from the class discussion.

Criteria for Assessment

- Clarity and depth of the personal fan narrative.

- Understanding and application of autoethnographic methods.

- Integration of scholarly perspectives with personal experience.

- Engagement and insights during the presentation and discussion.

- Quality of written reflection on the learning experience.

Throughout this exercise, students will not only delve into their personal attachments and histories within fandoms, but they will also contribute to a larger understanding of fan culture as a significant and complex social phenomenon with widespread social, psychological, cultural, and economic ramifications. This series of reflection exercises can be used as separate exercises or as one mega exercise. However it is adapted, it will allow students to gain a more personal and grounded appreciation of fandom and fandom relations as a unique lens through which to view their own lives and the world around them.

SOURCES

Amara, Mahfoud (2008), "The Muslim world in the global sporting arena," *The Brown Journal of World Affairs*, 14(2), 67-75.

Amenta, Edwin and Nathasha Miric (2013), "Sports Fandom," in Andrews, David L. and Ben Carrington (Eds.), *A Companion to Sport* (pp. 311-326). Blackwell.

Anselmo, Diana W. (2019), "Bound by Paper: Girl Fans, Movie Scrapbooks, and Hollywood Reception During World War I," *Film History*, 31(3, 141-172.

Arnold, Stephen J., and Eileen Fischer (1994), "Hermeneutics and consumer research." *Journal of Consumer Research*, 21(1), 55-70.

Arnould, Eric J., and Craig J. Thompson (2005), "Consumer culture theory (CCT): Twenty years of research." *Journal of Consumer Research*, 31(4), 868-882.

Atkins, Douglas (2004), *The Culting of Brands: Turn Your Customers into True Believers*. Portofolio Press.

Bacon-Smith, Camille (1992), *Enterprising Women: Television Fandom and the Creation of Popular Myth* (Philadelphia: University of Pennsylvania Press, 1992).

Baran, Sebnem (2024), "Populist Fandoms and Anti-fandoms: Politics, Polarization, and Celebritization in Turkey," *JCMS: Journal of Cinema and Media Studies*, 63 (2), 183-188.

Baulch, Emma (2004), "Reggae borderzones, reggae graveyards: Bob Marley fandom in Bali, "Perfect Beat: the Pacific journal of research into contemporary music and popular culture," 6(4), 3-27.

Baym, Nancy (2018), *Playing to the Crowd: Musicians, Audiences, and the Intimate Work of Connection*, New York: New York University Press.

Baym, Nancy, Daniel Cavicchi, and Norma Coates (2017), "Music fandom in the digital age: A conversation." In *The Routledge companion to media fandom*, (pp. 141-152). Routledge.

Becker, Howard (1982/2008), *Art Worlds* (25th Anniversary Edition), University of California Press.

Belk, Russell W., Melanie Wallendorf, and John F. Sherry Jr. (1989), "The sacred and the profane in consumer behavior: Theodicy on the odyssey." *Journal of Consumer Research*, 16 (1), 1-38.

Bielby, Denise D., and C. Lee Harrington (2004), "Managing culture matters: Genre, aesthetic elements, and the international market for exported television.: *Poetics,* 32(1), 73-98.

Booth, Paul (2010), *Digital fandom: New media studies.* Peter Lang.

Bordwell, David (1989), "A Case for Cognitivism," *Iris,* 9 (Spring), 11–40.

Borgerson, Janet L. (2014), "Materiality and the comfort of things: drinks, dining and discussion with Daniel Miller." In *Conversations on Consumption*, pp. 18-33. Routledge, 2014.

Borghini, Stefania, Nina Diamond, Robert V. Kozinets, Mary Ann McGrath, Albert Muniz, Jr., and John F. Sherry, Jr. (2009), "Why Are Themed Brandstores So Powerful? Retail Brand Ideology at American Girl Place," *Journal of Retailing*, 85 (September), 363-375.

Bourdieu, Pierre (1984), *Distinction: A social critique of the Judgement of Taste.* Harvard.

Branigan, Edward (1992) *Narrative Comprehension and Film* (London: Routledge).

Brown, Stephen, Robert V. Kozinets, and John F. Sherry, Jr. (2003a), "Sell Me the Old, Old Story: Retromarketing Management and the Art of Brand Revival," *Journal of Customer Behavior*, 2 (June), 85-98.

Brown, Stephen, Robert V. Kozinets, and John F. Sherry, Jr. (2003b), "Teaching Old Brands New Tricks: Retro Branding and the Revival of Brand Meaning," *Journal of Marketing*, 67 (July), 19-33.

Brown, Stephen (2007), "Harry Potter and the Fandom Menace," in *Consumer Tribes*, Bernard Cova, Robert V. Kozinets, and Avi Shankar, eds., Butterworth-Heinemann/ Elsevier, 177-193.

Brownlie, Douglas, Paul Hewer, and Steven Treanor (2007), "Sociality in motion: exploring logics of tribal consumption among cruisers." in *Consumer Tribes*, Bernard Cova, Robert V. Kozinets, and Avi Shankar, eds., Butterworth-Heinemann/ Elsevier, 109-128.

Bruns, Axel (2013), "From prosumption to produsage." In *Handbook on the Digital Creative Economy*, pp. 67-78. Edward Elgar Publishing.

Bury, Rhiannon (2018), ""We're not there": Fans, fan studies, and the participatory continuum." In Melissa A. Click and Suzanne Scott (Eds.), *The Routledge Companion to Media Fandom*, (pp. 123-131). Routledge.

Busse, Kristina (2013), "Geek hierarchies, boundary policing, and the gendering of the good fan," *Participations* 10 (1), 73-91.

Byrd, Jodi A (2014), "Tribal 2.0: Digital natives, political players, and the power of stories," *Studies in American Indian Literatures*, 26 (2), 55-64.

Carrington, Ben and David L. Andrews (2013), "Introduction: Sport as Escape, Struggle, and Art," in Andrews, David L. and Ben Carrington (Eds.), *A Companion to Sport* (pp. 1-16). Blackwell.

Case, Donald O. (2009), "Serial collecting as leisure, and coin collecting in particular." *Library Trends*, 57 (4), 729-752.

Cavicchi, Daniel (2014), "Fandom before "fan" shaping the history of enthusiastic audiences." *Reception: Texts, Readers, Audiences, History*, 6 (1), 52-72.

Choi, JungBong, and Roald Maliangkay (2014), "Introduction: Why fandom matters to the international rise of K-pop." In K-pop-the international rise of the Korean music industry, (pp. 1-18), Routledge.

Clark, Cory J., Brittany S. Liu, Bo M. Winegard, and Peter H. Ditto (2019), "Tribalism is human nature." *Current Directions in Psychological Science*, 28 (6), 587–592.

Corry, Jessica (2010), "The Beatles and the counterculture," *TCNJ Journal of Student Scholarship*, 8, 1-5.

Cova, Bernard, and Veronique Cova (2002), "Tribal marketing: The tribalisation of society and its impact on the conduct of marketing." *European Journal of Marketing*, 36 (5/ 6), 595-620.

Crawford, Garry (2003) "The career of the sport supporter: The case of the Manchester storm," *Sociology*, 37 (2), 219–237.

Culpepper, Mary Kay and David Gauntlett (2024), "The Construction of Everyday Creative Identity," *Journal of Creativity*, 34(2), https://doi.org/10.1016/j.yjoc.2024.100085

Davies, Callum, Bill Page, Carl Driesener, Zac Anesbury, Song Yang, and Johan Bruwer (2022), "The power of nostalgia: Age and preference for popular music," *Marketing Letters*, 33 (4), 681-692.

Davis, Erik (2005), *Led Zeppelin IV 33 ⅓*, New York: Continuum.

Dell, Chad (2006) *Revenge of Hatpin Mary: Women, Professional Wrestling and Fan Culture in the 1950s*, Peter Lange.

Dick, Philip K. (1962), *The Man in the High Castle*. G.P. Putnam's Sons.

Dick, Philip K. (1964), *The Three Stigmata of Palmer Eldritch*. Doubleday.

Dick, Philip K. (1969), *UBIK*. Doubleday.

Dick, Philip K. (1981), *VALIS*. Bantam.

Dietz-Uhler, Beth, and Jason R. Lanter (2008), "The consequences of sports fan identification." *Sports mania: Essays on fandom and the media in the 21st century*, 103-113.

Duffett, Mark (2000), "Transcending Audience Generalizations: Consumerism reconsidered in the case of Elvis Presley fans," *Popular Music & Society*, 24 (2), 75-91.

Edwards, Alexandra (2023), *Before Fan Fiction: Recovering the Literary History of American Media Fandom*, Louisiana State University Press.

Ehlert, Jennifer Bates (2018), "Hylas and the Matinée Girl: John William Waterhouse and the Female Gaze," *Athanor*, 36, 71-78.

Esmonde, Katelyn, Cheryl Cooky, and David L. Andrews (2015), ""It's supposed to be about the love of the game, not the love of Aaron Rodgers' eyes": Challenging the exclusions of women sports fans." *Sociology of Sport Journal*, 32 (1), 22-48.

Ferguson, Christine (2011), "Surface Tensions: Steampunk, Subculture, and the Ideology of Style." *Neo-Victorian Studies*, 4 (2), 66-90.

Firat, A. Fuat, and Alladi Venkatesh (1995), "Liberatory postmodernism and the reenchantment of consumption." *Journal of Consumer Research*, 22 (3), 239-267.

Fiske, John (1989; reprinted in 2010), "The Jeaning of America," *Understanding Popular Culture*, Routledge.

Fiske, John (1989; reprinted in 2010), *Understanding Popular Culture*, Routledge.

Flores, Andrew R., Donald P. Haider-Markel, Daniel C. Lewis, Patrick R. Miller, Barry L. Tadlock, and Jami K. Taylor (2020), "Public attitudes about transgender participation in sports: The roles of gender, gender identity conformity, and sports fandom," *Sex Roles*, 83, 382-398.

Fournier, Susan (1998), "Consumers and their brands: Developing relationship theory in consumer research." *Journal of Consumer Research*, 24 (4), 343-373.

Fozooni, Babak (2008), "Iranian Women and Football," *Cultural Studies*, 22 (1), 114-133.

Fyfe, Andy (2003), *When the Levee Breaks*, Chicago Review Press.

Fuller-Seeley, Kathryn (1996), *At the Picture Show: Small Town Audiences and the Creation of Movie Fan Culture*, Smithsonian.

Gantz, Walter, David Fingerhut, and Gayle Nadorff (2012), "The social dimension of sports fanship." in Earnheardt, Adam C., Haridakis, Paul M. and Barbara S. Hugenberg, eds. *Sports fans, identity, and socialization: Exploring the fandemonium*, (pp. 65077), Rowman & Littlefield.

Gantz, Walter, and Lawrence A. Wenner (1995), "Fanship and the television sports viewing experience." *Sociology of Sport Journal*, 12 (1), 56-74.

Gauntlett, David (2007) *Creative Explorations: New Approaches to Identities and Audiences,* Routledge.

Gauntlett, David (2018), *Making is connecting: The social power of creativity, from craft and knitting to digital everything*. John Wiley & Sons.

Gerrold, David (1973), *The World of Star Trek*. Ballantine Books.

Gerrold, David (1975), *The Trouble with Tribbles: The Complete Story of One of Star Trek's Most Popular Episodes*, Ballantine Books.

Giulianotti, Richard (2002), "Supporters, Followers, Fans, and Flâneurs: A Taxonomy of Spectator Identities in Football," *Journal of Sport and Social Issues*, 26 (1), 25–46.

Gould, Stephen J. (1991), "The Self-Manipulation of My Pervasive, Perceived Vital Energy through Product Use: An Introspective-Praxis Perspective," *Journal of Consumer Research*, 18 (2), 194-207.

Grossberg, Lawrence (1992), "Is there a fan in the house?: The affective sensibility of fandom." In Lewis, Lisa (Ed.), *The Adoring Audience* (pp. 50–65), Routledge.

Hains, Rebecca C., & Mazzarella, Sharon R., Eds. (2019), *Cultural Studies of LEGO: More than Just Bricks*. Palgrave Macmillan.

Hall, Stuart (1980), "Encoding/Decoding," *Culture, Media, Language*, Stuart Hall et al. (Eds.), (pp. 134-148), Hutchinson.

Hall, Stuart (2006). Notes on deconstructing 'the popular' In J. Storey, (Ed.), *Cultural Theory and Popular Culture* (3rd ed.). Pearson.

Halverson, Erica Rosenfeld, and Richard Halverson (2008), "Fantasy baseball: The case for competitive fandom," *Games and Culture*, 3 (3-4), 286-308.

Hayano, David M. (1979), "Auto-ethnography: Paradigms, problems, and prospects." *Human Organization,* 38(9), 99-104.

Hebdidge, Dick (1979), *Subculture: The Meaning of Style,* Routledge.

Heffernan, Kevin (2004). *Ghouls, Gimmicks, and Gold: Horror Films and The American Movie Business, 1953-1968.* Duke University Press.

Herbert, Frank (1965), *Dune.* Chilton Books.

Hewer, Paul, and Kathy Hamilton (2010), "On emotions and salsa: Some thoughts on dancing to rethink consumers." *Journal of Consumer Behaviour: An International Research Review,* 9(2), 113-125.

Hills, Matt (2002), *Fan Cultures.* Routledge.

Holbrook, Morris B., and Robert M. Schindler (1989), "Some exploratory findings on the development of musical tastes," *Journal of Consumer Research,* 16 (1), 119-124.

Horton, Donald, and R. Richard Wohl (1956), "Mass communication and para-social interaction: Observations on intimacy at a distance," *Psychiatry,* 19 (3), 215-229.

Huberman, Jenny (2012), "Forever a fan: Reflections on the branding of death and the production of value." *Anthropological Theory,* 12(4), 467-485.

Huang, Kerson and Rosemary Huang (1987), *I Ching.* Workman Publishing.

Hughson, John (1999), "A tale of two tribes: Expressive fandom in Australian Soccer's A-League," *Culture, Sport Society,* 2(3), 10-30.

Hunting, Kyra and Rebecca C. Hains, (2022), "'I'm Just Here to Enjoy the Ponies': My Little Pony, Bronies, and the Limits of Feminist Intent," *Popular Communication,* 20 (2), 38-151.

Jackson, Pamela, Jonathan Lethem, and Erik Davis, eds. (2011), *The Exegesis of Philip K. Dick.* Houghton Mifflin Harcourt.

Jenkins, Henry (1992), *Textual Poachers: Television Fans and Participatory Culture.* Routledge, Chapman and Hall.

Jenkins, Henry (1995), "'Do You Enjoy Making the Rest of Us Feel Stupid?': alt.tv.twinpeaks," the Trickster Author and Viewer Mastery" in David Lavery (ed.) *Full of Secrets: Critical Approaches to Twin Peaks,* Wayne State University Press.

Jenkins, Henry (2007), "Death-Defying Heroes," in Sherry Turkle (ed.) *Evocative Objects: Things We Think With,* MIT University Press.

Jenkins, Henry (2008), *Convergence Culture: Where Old and New Media Collide,* New York University Press.

Jenkins, Henry (2011) "Why John Fiske (Still) Matters," introduction included in second edition reprint of Fiske's *Understanding Popular Culture, Reading the Popular, Introduction to Communications,* and *Television Culture,* Routledge.

Jenkins, Henry (2012), "I Was a (Pre)Teenage Monster," *Journal of Fandom Studies,* 1 (1), 87-100.

Jenkins, Henry (2016) "Raymond Williams and John Fiske," in Renee Hobbs (ed.) *Exploring the Roots of Digital and Media Literacy Through Personal Narrative,* Temple University Press.

Jenkins, Henry, Sam Ford, and Joshua Green (2013) *Spreadable Media: Creating Meaning and Value in a Networked Culture,* New York University Press.

Jenkins, Mizuko Ito, and danah boyd (2015), *Participatory Culture in a Networked Era,* Polity.

Jenkins, Henry, Erica Rand, and Karen Helleckson, (2011), "Acafandom and Beyond," *Pop Junctions* (originally *Confessions of an Aca-Fan*), June 20, available at http://henryjenkins.org/blog/2011/06/acafandom_and_beyond_week_two.html

Jenkins, Henry, Sangita Sreshtova, Liana Gambler-Thompson, Neta Kligler-Vilinchek, and Arley Zimmerman (2016) *By Any Media Necessary: The New Youth Activism,* New York University Press.

Joseph, Franz (1975), *Star Fleet Technical Manual,* Ballantine Books.

Kashima, Yoshi, Olivier Klein, and Anna E. Clark (2007), "Grounding: Sharing information in social interaction." In K. Fielder (Ed.), *Social Communication* (pp. 27–77), Psychology Press.

Kim, Hun Shik (2016), "The Korean Wave as soft power public diplomacy." In Naren Chitty et al. (Eds.), *The Routledge Handbook of Soft Power,* (pp. 434-444), Routledge.

King, S and Jensen, R. (1996), "Bob Marley's 'Redemption Song': The Rhetoric of Reggae and Rastafari', *Journal of Popular Culture* v29n3: 17-36.

Koestler, Arthur (1978), *Janus: A Summing Up,* New York: Random House.

Kozinets, Robert V. (1999), "E-Tribalized Marketing? The Strategic Implications of Virtual Communities of Consumption," *European Management Journal,* 17 (3), 252-264.

Kozinets, Robert V. (2001), "Utopian Enterprise: Articulating the Meanings of Star Trek's Culture of Consumption," *Journal of Consumer Research,* 28 (June), 67-88.

Kozinets, Robert V. (2002), "The Field Behind the Screen: Using Netnography for Marketing Research in Online Communities," *Journal of Marketing Research*, 39 (February), 61-72.

Kozinets, Robert V. (2007), "Inno-tribes: Star Trek as Wikimedia," in *Consumer Tribes*, Bernard Cova, Robert V. Kozinets, and Avi Shankar, eds., Oxford: Butterworth-Heinemann/Elsevier, 194-211.

Kozinets, Robert V. (2010), "Brand Fans: When Entertainment + Marketing Intersect on the Net," in Tracey Tuten, ed. *Enterprise 2.0: How Technology, E-Commerce, and Web 2.0 Are Transforming Business Virtually*, Volume 2, Santa Barbara, CA: Praeger, 145-166.

Kozinets, Robert V. (2014), "Fan Creep: Why Brands Suddenly Need 'Fans,'" in Denise Mann ed., *Wired TV: Post-Network Television's Virtual Worlds*, New York: Rutgers University Press, 161-175.

Kozinets, Robert V. and Jay M. Handelman (1998) "Ensouling Consumption: A Netnographic Exploration of The Meaning of Boycotting Behavior," in *Advances in Consumer Research*, Volume 25, ed., Joseph Alba and Wesley Hutchinson, Provo, UT: Association for Consumer Research, 475-480.

Kozinets, Robert V. and Jay M. Handelman (2004), "Adversaries of Consumption: Consumer Movements, Activism, and Ideology," *Journal of Consumer Research*, 31 (December), 691-704.

Kozinets, Robert V., and Henry Jenkins (2022), "Consumer movements, brand activism, and the participatory politics of media: A conversation." *Journal of Consumer Culture*, 22 (1), 264-282.

Kozinets, Robert V., Sherry, John F., Jr., Diana Storm, Adam Duhachek, Krittinee Nuttavuthisit, and Benét DeBerry-Spence (2002), "Themed Flagship Brand Stores in the New Millennium: Theory, Practice, Prospects," *Journal of Retailing*, 78 (Spring), 17-29.

Kozinets, Robert V., John F. Sherry, Jr., Diana Storm, Adam Duhachek, Krittinee Nuttavuthisit, and Benét DeBerry-Spence (2004), "Ludic Agency and Retail Spectacle," *Journal of Consumer Research*, 31 (December), 658-672.

Lacasa, Pilar, Julián de la Fuente, Maria Garcia-Pernia, and Sara Cortes (2017), "Teenagers, fandom and identity." *Persona Studies*, 3(2), 51-65.

Langer, Roy (2007), "Marketing, prosumption, and innovation in the fetish community," in *Consumer Tribes*, Bernard Cova, Robert V. Kozinets, and Avi Shankar, eds., Oxford: Butterworth-Heinemann/Elsevier, pp. 252-268.

Lawrence, Stefan, and Christian Davis (2019),. "Fans for diversity? A Critical Race Theory analysis of Black, Asian and Minority Ethnic (BAME) supporters' experiences of fandom," *International Journal of Sport Policy and Politics*, 11 (4), 701-713.

Lee, Stan (1974), *Origins of Marvel Comics*, New York: Simon and Schuster.

Lee, Stan (1975), *Son of Origins of Marvel Comics*, New York: Simon and Schuster.

Lee, Stan, and John Buscema (1984), *How to Draw Comics the Marvel Way*, New York: Simon and Schuster.

Leonardi, Paul M. (2010), "Digital materiality? How artifacts without matter, matter." *First monday* (2010).

Lewis, Lisa (1992) *The Adoring Audience: Fan Culture and Popular Media*, London: Routledge.

Lewis, Nicky, and Walter Gantz (2019), "An online dimension of sports fanship: Fan activity on NFL team-sponsored websites." *Journal of Global Sport Management*, 4 (3), 257-270.

Lichtenberg, Jacqueline, Sondra Marshak, and Joan Winston (1975), *Star Trek Lives!*, New York: Bantam Books.

Lichter-Marck, Rose (2016), "Eyes aloft: The sublime obsession of plane spotting." *The Virginia Quarterly Review*, 92 (4), 52-63.

Lloyd, Annemaree, and Michael Olsson (2019), "Enacting and capturing embodied knowledge in the practices of enthusiast car restorers: Emerging themes." *Journal of Librarianship and Information Science* 51 (4), 1033-1040.

Loy, John and Coakley, Jay (2007), "Sport," in Ritzer, George (Ed.) *The Blackwell Encyclopedia of Sociology* (pp. 317-321), Blackwell.

Lucas, George (1977), *Star Wars: From the Adventures of Luke Skywalker*. New York: Ballantine Books.

Luedicke, Marius K., and Markus Giesler (2007), "Brand communities and their social antagonists: insights from the Hummer case," in *Consumer Tribes*, Bernard Cova, Robert V. Kozinets, and Avi Shankar (Eds.), Butterworth-Heinemann/ Elsevier, 275-95.

Maffesoli, Michel (1996), *The Time of the Tribes: The Decline of Individualism in Mass Society*, London: SAGE.

Markovits, Andrei S. and Steven L. Hellerman (2001), *Offside: Soccer and American Exceptionalism*, Princeton.

Martin, Alfred L. (2019), "Fandom while black: Misty Copeland, Black Panther, Tyler Perry and the contours of US black fandoms." *International Journal of Cultural Studies*, 22(6), 737-753.

Mattel / no author attribution (1969), *Welcome to Upsy Downsy Land*. Racine, WI: Western Publishing Company.

McCarron, Owen (1976), *The Mighty Marvel Superheroes Fun Book*, New York: Simon and Schuster.

McCracken, Grant (1986), "Culture and consumption: A theoretical account of the structure and movement of the cultural meaning of consumer goods." *Journal of Consumer Research*, 13 (1), 71-84.

McRobbie, Angela (1991), "Settling Accounts with Subcultures: A Feminist Account," *Feminism and Youth Culture: From Jackie to Just Seventeen* (Springer) http://www.hu.mtu.edu/~jdslack/readings/CSReadings/McRobbie_Settling_Accounts_with_Subcultures.pdf.

Mendonca, Marlene Ramos (2018), *Archiving the "Sweet" Candy-Loving Matinee Girl:*

Fashion, Confectionaries, and Fan Scrapbooking in Urban American Culture, 1880-1915, Theater and Performance Studies, York University.

Mercier, Faye (2022), "'Maybe if she stanned…': Reinforcing fan identities and affirming positive fan-object relations through toxic practices in K-Pop fandom." *Journal of Fandom Studies*, 10, no. 2-3 (2022): 199-221.

Messerlin, Patrick A., and Wonkyu Shin (2017), "The success of K-pop: How Big and why so fast?" *Asian Journal of Social Science*, 45 (4-5), 409-439.

Mihailidus, Paul, Sangita Shresthova, and Megan Fromme, Eds. (2021), *Transformative Media Pedagogies*, Routledge.

Muñiz Jr, Albert M., and Thomas C. O'Guinn (2001), "Brand community." *Journal of Consumer Research*, 27(4), 412-432.

Obsession Inc. (2009), "Affirmational Fandom vs. Transformational Fandom." *Dreamwidth*, 1 Jun. 2009. Accessed 10 Apr. 2024 <https://obsession-inc.dreamwidth.org/82589.html>.

O'Gormon, Pamela (1997), "On Reggae and Rastafarianism – and a Garvey prophesy" in Chris Potash (Ed.) *Reggae, Rasta, Revolution: Jamaican music from Ska to Dub*, (pp. 255-258), Schirmer Books:

Murray, Janet (1997), *Hamlet on the Holodeck: The Future of Narrative in Cyberspace*, Free Press.

Oh, Ingyu, and Gil-Sung Park (2013), "The globalization of K-pop: Korea's place in the global music industry," *Korea Observer*, 44(3), 389-409.

Onion, Rebecca (2008), "Reclaiming the Machine: An Introductory Look at Steampunk in Everyday Practice," *Neo-Victorian Studies*, 1 (1), 138-163

Oren, Tasha (2023), *Food TV*, Routledge.

Otnes, Cele C., and Maclaran, Pauline (2007), "The consumption of cultural heritage among a British Royal Family brand tribe," in *Consumer Tribes*, Bernard Cova, Robert V. Kozinets, and Avi Shankar, eds., Oxford: Butterworth-Heinemann/Elsevier, 49-65.

Park, David J., Sameer Deshpande, Bernard Cova, and Stefano Pace (2007), "Seeking community through battle: understanding the meaning of consumption processes for Warhammer gamers' communities across borders," in *Consumer Tribes*, Bernard Cova, Robert V. Kozinets, and Avi Shankar, eds., Oxford: Butterworth-Heinemann/Elsevier, 212-223. Elsevier.

Parry, Jim, and Jacob Giesbrecht (2023), "Esports, real sports, and the Olympic Virtual Series." *Journal of the Philosophy of Sport*, 50(2), 208-228.

Penley, Constance (1991), "Feminism, Psychoanalysis, and the Study of Popular Culture," in Lawrence Grosberg, Cary Nelson, and Paula A. Treichler (eds.), *Cultural Studies*, Durham: Duke University Press.

Peters-Lozario, Gabriel and Sangita Shresthova (2021), *Practicing Futures: A Civic Imagination Action Handbook*. Peter Lange.

Pratt, Mary Louise (1991), "Arts of the Contact Zone," *Profession*, pp. 33-40.

Punathambeker, Aswin (2007) "Between Rowdies and Rasikas: Rethinking Fan Activity in Indian Fan Culture" in Jonathan Gray, Cornel Sanvoss and C. Lee Harrington (eds.) *Fandom: Identities and Communities in a Mediated World* (New York: New York University Press)

Radway, Janice (1991) *Reading the Romance: Women, Patriarchy and Popular Literature* (Chapel Hill: University of North Carolina Press).

Rai, Swampnil (2019) "'May the Force Be with You': Narendra Modi and th Celebritization of Indian Politics", *Communication, Culture and Critique*, 19, 323-339.

Rai, Swapnil (2023) *Networked Bollywood: How Star Power Globalized Hindi Cinema*. Cambridge University.

Rai, Swapnil and Brandy Monk-Payton (2024), "In Focus Introduction: The Celebritization of Politics in Global Media Culture," *JCMS*, 63(2), 144–148

Reist, Nancy (1997), "Counting Stars by Candlelight: An Analysis of the Mythic Appeal of the Grateful Dead," *Journal of Popular Culture*, 30 (4), 183-209.

Reysen, Stephen, and Nyla R. Branscombe (2010), Fanship and fandom: Comparisons between sport and non-sport fans." *Journal of Sport Behavior*, 33 (2), 176-193.

Rohr, Nicolette (2017), "Yeah yeah yeah: The sixties screamscape of Beatlemania," *Journal of Popular Music Studies*, 29 (2), e12213.

Rose, Frank (2012), *The Art of Immersion: How the Digital Generation Is Remaking Hollywood, Madison Avenue, and the Way We Tell Stories*. New York: W.W. Norton.

Salmi, Hannu (2020), "Emotional Contagions: Franz Liszt and the materiality of Celebrity Culture in the 1830s and 1840s." in Hillard, Derek, Lempa, Heikki, and Russell Spinney (Eds.)

Feelings Materialized—Emotions, Bodies, and Things in Germany, 1500–1950, (pp. 61-91), Berghahn Books).

Sackett, Susan (1977), *Letters to Star Trek*, New York: Ballantine Books.

Sandvoss, Cornel (2005), *Fans: The Mirror of Consumption*. Polity Press.

Schau, Hope Jensen, and Albert M. Muñiz Jr. (2007), "Temperance and religiosity in a non-marginal, non-stigmatized brand community," in *Consumer Tribes*, Bernard Cova, Robert V. Kozinets, and Avi Shankar, eds., Oxford: Butterworth-Heinemann/ Elsevier, 144-62.

Scott, David Meerman, and Brian Halligan (2010), *Marketing Lessons from the Grateful Dead: What every business can learn from the most iconic band in history*. John Wiley & Sons.

Sherry, John F., Jr., Robert V. Kozinets, Diana Storm, Adam Duhachek, Krittinee Nuttavuthisit and Benét DeBerry-Spence (2001), "Being In The Zone: Staging Retail Theater at ESPN Zone Chicago," *Journal of Contemporary Ethnography*, 30 (August), 465-510.

Sherry, John F., Jr., Robert V. Kozinets, Adam Duhachek, Benét DeBerry-Spence, Krittinee Nuttavuthisit and Diana Storm (2004), "Gendered Behavior in a Male Preserve: Role Playing at ESPN Zone Chicago," *Journal of Consumer Psychology*, 14 (1 & 2), 151-158.

Shrethsova, Sangita (2011), Is *It All About the Hips?: Around the World with Bollywood Dance* (London: Sage)

Shrethsova, Sangita (2020) "Moving to a Bollywood Beat, "Born in the USA" Goes

My Indian Heart? Exploring Possibility and Imagination through Hindi Film Dance" in Henry Jenkins, Gabriel Peters-Lazaro and Sangita Shresthova (Eds.) *Popular Culture and the Civic Imagination: Case Studies of Creative Social Change*, New York University Press.

Solomon, Michael R., and Henry Assael (1987), "The forest or the trees?: A gestalt approach to symbolic consumption." In Michael Solomon, Ed., *Marketing and semiotics: New directions in the study of signs for sale* (pp. 189-218), De Gruyter Mouton.

Sontag, Susan (1975) "Fascinating Fascism," *New York Review of Books,* February 6, 1975

Stanfill, Mel (2018), "The unbearable whiteness of fandom and fan studies,"in Paul Booth (Ed.), *A Companion to Media Fandom and Fan Studies* (pp. 305-317), John Wioley & Sons.

Stebbins, Robert A. (1982), "Serious leisure: A conceptual statement," *Pacific Sociological Review*, 25(2), 251-272.

Stein, Louisa Ellen, and Kristina Busse (2012), "Introduction: The Literary, Televisual, and Digital Adventures of the Beloved Detective," in Louisa Ellen Stein and Kristina Busse (eds.), *Sherlock and Transmedia Fandom: Essays on the BBC Series* (Jefferson: McFarland and Company).

Tajfel, Henri (1978), *Differentiation Between Social Groups: Studies in the Social Psychology of Intergroup Relations*, Academic Press.

Tinson, Julie, Gary Sinclair, and Dimitrios Kolyperas (2017), "Sport fandom and parenthood." *European Sport Management Quarterly*, 17 (3), 370-391.

Toffler, Alvin (1980), *The Third Wave: The Classic Study of Tomorrow*. New York: Bantam.

Trimble, Bjo (1976), *Star Trek Concordance*, New York: Ballantine.

Tsuji, Izumi (2012), "Why Study Train Otaku?: A Social History of the Imagination" in izuko Ito, Daisuke Okabe, Izumi Tsuji (Eds.) *Fandom Unbound: Otaku Culture in a Connected World* (New Haven: Yale University Press).

Tulloch, John and Henry Jenkins (1995), *Science Fiction Audiences: Watching Star Trek and Doctor Who*, Routledge.

Tzu, Lao (1998), *Tao Te Ching: A Book about the Way and the Power of the Way*. Trans., Ursula K. Le Guin, Boston: Shambhala.

Wanzo, Rebecca (2015), "African American Acafandom and Other Strangers: New Genealogies of Fan Studies," *Transformative Works and Cultures*, 20, https://doi.org/10.3983/twc.2015.0699.

Williams, Rebecca (2021), *Theme Park Fandom: Spatial Transmedia, Materiality and Participatory Fandom*, Amsterdam: Amsterdam University Press.

Wolf, Michael J. (1999), *The Entertainment Economy: How Mega-Media Forces are Transforming Our Lives*, Three Rivers Press.

YouGov (2022), "Global Sports 2022: Uncovering the Socially Responsible Sports Fan," White Paper, YouGov.

Zirin, Dave (2010), *Bad Sports: How Owners are Ruining the Games We Love*. Simon and Schuster.

INDEX

www.ingramcontent.com/pod-product-compliance
Lightning Source LLC
Chambersburg PA
CBHW072127270326
41931CB00010B/1695